THE NEXT GIG

Frank Kelly

The Next Gig

CURRACH
PRESS

First published in 2015 by
CURRACH PRESS
55A Spruce Avenue,
Stillorgan Industrial Park,
Blackrock, Co. Dublin

Cover design by Helene Pertl / Currach Press
Cover image by Emmet Bergin
Origination by Currach Press
Printed by ScandBook AB, Sweden

ISBN 978 1 78218 840 7

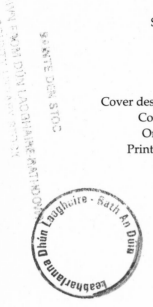

For Bairbre, forever.

Foreword

by Fergus Linehan

It's so long ago now that I can't remember exactly when I first met Frank Kelly. I know it was some time back in the 1950s. We were both students in UCD, putting on much acclaimed revues in the Aula Maxima in Stephen's Green. We were a talented bunch, or so we liked to think. My future wife, Rosaleen Linehan, and Des Keogh both went on to careers on stage and screen, as did Frank. From the word go it was obvious we had a pearl of rare price in Frank, who could act and sing well, play the fiddle and, above all, was a wonderfully funny guy. This is his own story of growing up, and of the many people and places he has encountered while, with his wife Bairbre, bringing up a large and lively family.

Frank grew up in Blackrock, a very different place from the well-manicured, densely populated suburb it is now. There were open fields with little streams running through them, farms and an almost rural feel to it then. Frank's father, Charlie Kelly, was something of a celebrity, a founder of the comic magazine *Dublin Opinion* and for many years head of Radio Éireann.

The Kellys were a large family, of which Frank was the youngest. Like many of us who ended up, in one form or another, attached to the 'painted stage', he was something of a cuckoo in the nest, failing exams and generally behaving like a troubled adolescent. It was only when he got into UCD that he found his true pathway in life. After a few diversions, when he qualified as a barrister and worked in journalism, he embarked full-time on the career for which he is now so well known.

Meanwhile he had married Bairbre, a very young widow with two little girls. They went on to have five other children. The Kellys never did anything by halves! Fortunately too, Bairbre has always been a wonderful wife and mother; warm, supportive and, having acted herself, deeply involved in 'the business'.

Despite its often spurious glamour, the life of most actors can be hard, even without a large brood to raise. The pay is bad, the profession is always overcrowded and work conditions can be rotten. Frank has always faced this with great courage and, though inevitably there have been hard times, he has come through them triumphantly. It could be said that he has been a household name not once but twice and that his career covers every aspect of theatre, film, radio and television in Ireland.

He first made himself known to a larger public through his work in the early days of television here, in programmes such as the comedy show *Hall's Pictorial Weekly* and the children's series *Wanderly Wagon*. But that wasn't the half of it. Around the same time he was doing radio comedy, cabaret, 'legit' roles for Hilton Edwards and Micheál MacLiammóir at the Gate Theatre, film work and variety with comedians like Jimmy O'Dea and Jack Cruise. Indeed, there hardly seemed a type of entertainment around but Frank turned up in it.

All this couldn't go on forever, of course, and there were times when the phone didn't ring. But somehow or other, Frank kept going. He travelled the country doing cabaret, toured Middle America with the plays of John B. Keane and took parts that were unworthy of him. He was the great survivor.

Then, out of the blue, came what I think of as his second stint as a household name. No one could have anticipated the huge success that *Father Ted* enjoyed during the 1990s. The much-cherished show continues to entertain to this day, with Frank at his comic best as the awful geriatric Fr Jack. Anyone who has ever seen it is not going to forget this horrible but hilarious old cleric.

Frank continues to pop up in the most surprising places. He has done a stint in the soap *Emmerdale*, toured the Scottish Highlands, and even played a (non-singing) role at the Glyndebourne Opera Festival. He and Bairbre have fought the good fight and raised a great family of many children and grandchildren. At his most recent performance, in John B. Keane's *Moll* at the Gaiety Theatre, the audience burst into spontaneous applause when he first came on stage. It was a measure of the admiration and affection we all feel for him and which this book illustrates so well. Encore!

Thank you to my beloved family,
who helped so much in the production of this book.

Contents

---— 1 —---

War Babies

My family were all 'war babies'. In an Irish context this means that you were born just a few years before, or just at the outbreak of, the last world war, so that the earliest topics you heard discussed were 'The Gerries', 'The Allies', and rationing. For most war babies, looking back to that time, there is a feeling that somehow when the war ended, everything became brighter. It was as though the lights had been dimmed until then; that everything had been sepia-coloured.

After the war, there seemed to be vistas of hope and brightness, and even as a very small child – although you couldn't be aware of something so complex as this – you sensed the change in your parents and aunties and uncles.

We were called in from playing in the garden to taste our first oranges, and to see our first lemons, and this seemed to mark the beginning of the end of the austerity of war for our parents. There was still rationing for a couple of years after the war but it was relaxed gradually.

Only a limited number of people were allowed access to petrol, for a few years, such as doctors and commercial travellers, and so there was little motorised transport on the roads. Our Morris Cowley motor car was kept up on blocks, and we would climb into it and go for imaginary journeys in the garage for hours on end.

Delivery men from the bakeries and dairies travelled from house to house on their horse-drawn carts, and the more daring young bloods would cling to the back of the bakery vans, until removed by flicks of the driver's whip, which he used with great casts, like a salmon fisherman, while staring straight ahead. This meant that, should anyone be injured, he could claim to have been unaware that he was carrying an unwanted passenger.

In Dublin city there were horse-drawn cabs, which made their way along all the main thoroughfares. I remember my mother, humming and hawing, deciding whether it would be worth her taking a cab or not, and the sheer joy when she decided to hail one, and the rumble of the wheels on the cobbles.

This memory gives one the sensation of having lived in a much earlier Dublin, such as that of James Joyce. The lack of petrol seemed to take society back in time to a different pattern of living. People walked and cycled a great deal, and the view of their city and suburbs was not obscured by constant flows of motor traffic.

Things which we now take for granted, like white sugar, were unobtainable. I remember sneaking into our pantry where my mother had collected brown sugar in hessian sacks, and running my hands over them. The outsides were sticky from the sugar seeping through slightly, and I would lick the palms of my hands in ecstacy.

Eggs were very scarce. I imagine that they were being exported to England. When I was very small, you were never given a whole fried egg. You got half an egg, and you didn't dare to complain. These food scarcities were quite formative in your early education, because you were being constantly reminded of the suffering of the people in Europe, devastated by war, and thus complaining and whingeing were out of the question.

My mother used to preserve eggs in a colourless jelly, called water glass, in basins and buckets, and it was quite some time after the war that I got a whole fried egg.

Bread was a depressing grey colour, and not very appetising. Eating it was a chore. And then came 'white bread', which was manna to our young palates, and I have been a 'breadaholic' ever since.

One big puzzle for me was that when we were called in for our 'tea', we were given cocoa. I thought that adults had lost the plot altogether. And then tea ceased to be rationed and we got the real thing, which we called 'real tea'. For about a year after it ceased to be rationed, tea was called 'real tea' in our house, until my mother told us that we would be disgraced if anyone outside the family heard us talking about 'real tea'.

It has been said by many that, unlike English children, Irish children never heard the sound of enemy aircraft overhead, but I have checked with my siblings, and we all remembered the difference between the sound of an English squadron of aircraft passing down the east coast, and a German one. The German one had a deep 'thrum-thrum-thrum' sound, and the British one was much higher. I don't think that the imagination of each one of us could have invented this memory independently. The coincidence would be just too great.

When we were small, we played with our gas masks until they were reclaimed by the authorities. Every house was issued with a gas mask for each member of the family by the Irish ARP service (Air Raid Precaution), and hence the rhyme of the time to which we all danced around and sang:

> Underneath the spreading chestnut tree
> De Valera said to me:
> 'If you want to get your gas mask free,
> Join the Irish ARP.'

There was also a device issued called 'a stirrup pump', which you placed in a bucket of water, on to the lip of a bucket, with a contraption for pumping with the foot on the outside. This produced a prodigious jet of water. It isn't surprising that they were retrieved with such alacrity after the war, because it would have been so tempting to hold on to them for chores like washing the car or hosing down paths.

Insofar as the east coast was nearer to Britain than the rest of the country, there was a feeling among people like my parents that the threat of war was more imminent than elsewhere in the country, and arrangements were made for children like me to be evacuated to rural destinations. Fortunately the necessity for this never arose.

— 2 —

West Britain

I was born in Blackrock, just five miles south of Dublin city, in Ireland. Blackrock was a stage on what was a military road in Napoleonic times, and for over a hundred years it was used for marching British troops to the city, after disembarkation at Dún Laoghaire, and earlier at Coliemore Harbour, in Dalkey. The city sported Dublin Castle, seat of the British administration in Ireland. Thus, from early times, when the Pale was drawn, cutting off Leinster from the rest of Ireland, our area became known as 'West Britain'.

This tag stuck to us as children, and probably still does. There is a connotation in it of being slightly less 'Irish' than someone from Limerick or Galway, and as a taxpayer and native Irishman, I have always resented this perception. One distinguishing mark of the Pale was the absence of spoken Irish, which made it extremely difficult for us to retain what we learned of the language, because no one around us spoke it. You cannot continue to speak a language in a vacuum. There has to be immersion. The Irish for West Britons was the derisory term, 'Seoinín', almost invariably hurled by someone who revelled in the supreme achievement of happening to have been born somewhere where Irish was spoken, or taught in a better way.

Blackrock and the surrounding districts were relics of the old British Empire, where the few who owned much of Irish industry, and those who had retired from careers in exotic climes, lived in beautiful villas, well listed in Peter Pearson's book, *Between the Mountains and The Sea*. The colonial influence is still to be seen in gardens which sport eucalyptus trees and plants brought back from places like Malaya (modern day Malaysia).

I have a clear memory of calling at a house in Blackrock at Halloween to beg for apples and nuts, only to be confronted by a genuinely bewildered householder who said: 'But it's not Guy Fawke's night yet. I'm afraid you've got your date wrong, young man.'

Frescati House, summer home of the Duke of Leinster's family, of Carton Demesne, Maynooth, where Lord Edward Fitzgerald hid while on the run, stood roughly where the Frascati Centre stands today, but was there in all its fading glory in my youth, and I played in it many times. As children, we encountered a man there, named Farquharson, who had retired from the Malayan Police Service, and who presented us with his baton and rattle. The house was demolished overnight by developers to make way for the shopping centre development. Nobody was held properly accountable for the demolition of this priceless piece of history.

On Temple Road, which runs behind the St John the Baptist Church, stood a pub called The Three Tun, owned by one Timothy Murphy and which dated back to the seventeenth century. This ancient inn should never have been altered in character, and in England, would be a carefully preserved, listed building, but it changed hands many times, and has lost all of its original character. There is no criticism intended of the various, successive owners since Tim Murphy's day. They were trying to do what they thought their business needed, but with encouragement and the right advice and access to funding, the village might have had a real treasure.

When we were children, these villas, bastions of colonialism, were guarded by 'The Man'. 'The Man' was a curious breed of individual, with a blind loyalty to his (probably) indifferent employer, who was paid a pittance to guard His Lordship's parklands like a hungry Rottweiler. There were generally orchards, from which to steal apples (a practice known as 'boxing the fox'), and the delicious prospect of a damned good chase from 'The Man'. If you were caught by 'The Man', you might get a drubbing, but this rarely happened, because the kind of boys who 'boxed the fox' were pretty daring and agile, and sheer terror is great sauce.

Sometimes 'The Man' had the dubious privilege of living in a damp hovel on the land, but most of these have disappeared over the years, as, sadly, have many of the villas.

There were many damp cottages, up mossy lanes behind fine houses, where 'working class' people lived, and most of these, too, have disappeared. They were occupied by live-in gardeners and men who served with the British Forces, and have been obliterated by the vast housing developments in the area.

These men, serving with the British troops, used to come back on leave, with money to spend, and would stagger home from the pubs in Blackrock village in a highly drunken state. I have clear memories of them falling repeatedly up Avoca Avenue, towards Stillorgan village and the aforementioned damp cottages, and on one occasion seeing a drunken man, with his face literally covered with blood, from where it had struck the road several times. It is likely that their bellies hadn't been too full of food.

Blackrock sported an open sea baths of some splendour, which was a much used municipal amenity, and stood behind the railway station, being reached by a bridge across the line. It was maintained in the best of condition by Dún Laoghaire Borough Corporation workers, who were really dedicated to the task. It was mainly identifiable by its ten-metre-high diving platform, to be seen from the station's car park. The whole place was painted a gleaming white, which gave it a festive air in the summer sun.

The ballroom reigned supreme after the war as a centre of entertainment, and Blackrock sported its own, The Lido, which also incorporated an ice-cream parlour and sweetshop.

This was the Blackrock into which I was born. I was brought home from The Leinster Nursing Home to No. 14, Mount Merrion

Avenue to join my two brothers and three sisters. My poor mother had six children in seven years, of which I was the youngest. Next in line above me were the twins, my brother David and my sister Pauline, then my sisters Brenda and Mary Rose, and my brother Aidan, eldest in the family.

One of the big attractions advertised by the vendors of the house was the fact that there was a nice little river running behind it. This will show readers the ambience of Blackrock at that time. No one nowadays would consider a small river to be an attraction; rather, they might see it as a source of attraction to rats. Much building has been done behind the house now. There is a fine block of apartments, and I'm sure the river has been culverted.

Mind you, the river did have its day one winter, when it rose in all its glory, near Hyde Park Avenue, halfway up Mount Merrion Avenue, and burst through the wall, running unhindered all the way to the gates of Blackrock Park, and down a steep slope, taking away all the flower beds on its way to the waterway beside the railway. It was a most impressive rebellion, as it also tore up all the tarmacadam surface of the avenue, which stuck up into the air in great slabs, like the aftermath of an earthquake.

All we could think of, as children, was: 'Three cheers for the river!' However, it was soon taught manners, and contained in a way which would prevent it from ever rebelling again. There is something satisfying about nature showing its ancient muscles now and then.

When my mother arrived in Blackrock as a bride, she was what was then known as a 'flapper girl'. These were slender little girls, who wore cloche hats and looked as though they were about to dance the charleston. She was blue-eyed and blonde, and light as a feather, but after having six children in seven years she lost her figure forever, and spent the rest of her life trying to get it back, as evidenced by the remains of so many dietary regimes to be found in our kitchen presses until she died. She used to tell a tale of how she was down in Blackrock Park with one of us as a baby, when she used the toilet facility in a pavilion near the main gates, which was manned by a pleasant woman, of whom I have a dim memory. They chatted for a while, and my mother made some rueful remark about her own figure.

The woman reassured her with: 'Ah sure Missus, I wouldn't worry myself if I were you. There was a lovely little lady who moved into one of the houses just up the road there only a few years ago, and when she came here she was the slimmest little thing ye ever saw, and then she had a clatter of kids, and ye'd want to see her now. Her lovely figure is gone completely!' The woman hadn't recognised my mother as the heroine of her story, and my mother headed home somewhat chastened.

To her great credit, she often told the story, and was able to laugh at the irony, but then her sense of humour was to prove itself to be her salvation many times, when her life seemed to be at its darkest. The location was a good one to rear a 'clatter of kids'.

On the corner of Mount Merrion Avenue and Cross Avenue was Sion Hill Dominican Convent, in whose kindergarten we all began our education, the girls progressing right through the school, and the boys going to Willow Park, the preparatory school for Black-rock College, after making our First Communion.

My father, Charles E. Kelly, must have been a very ambitious young man. I remember Felim, his youngest brother, a Passionist priest who took the name 'Honorius' in the religious life (for some reason this name always made me smirk as a child), telling me that when my parents moved into No. 14, Mount Merrion Avenue, it was as though they had bought a place on the Riviera in the eyes of those who lived in the small terrace of houses in Harold's Cross, where he came from.

His father had attended the old Royal University, but had not completed his studies for family reasons, and held the grand title of 'Corporation Official'. He wore a bowler hat, a high stiff collar, and sported a carefully waxed moustache.

—∿— 3 —∿—

Upwardly Mobile

In spite of having six children in seven years, my father managed to purchase a beautiful mansion, Rosemount, in Avoca Avenue, Blackrock, which had twelve rooms, two garages, a beautiful sunken front lawn, and an orchard at the back. His income from the civil service and *Dublin Opinion*, a humorous magazine which he co-edited, and had founded with two friends, would hardly have stretched to that.

Also, he didn't sell No. 14, Mount Merrion Avenue, but let it after we had moved. I can only conclude that he was what was known as a 'bankable' young man, and going places. In those days bank managers had more discretion than nowadays, and really had close personal knowledge of the person with whom they were banking.

At that time the whole Blackrock area was quite different from the series of housing estates and apartment blocks which it is today. Much of it consisted of big dairy farms. I well remember the names: Acres (an apt name for a dairyman), Mooney's and Morrows. Much of the area consisted of open fields. Carysfort Convent owned all the land which stretched from Avoca Avenue to Stillorgan, and beyond to St Augustine's School for special children.

At the top of Avoca Avenue, there were the remains of the entrance to what had been an old priory, in whose ruins I often played. It had considerable lands, which ran all the way to the Stillorgan Road. Indeed its avenue and park still retain the prefix 'priory' to this day.

When we were children my mother used to take us blackberry-picking from beyond the old wooden church at Mount Merrion, all the way to Goatstown, over a series of muddy paths. There were no Mount Merrion housing estates, just virgin fields, apart from The Rise and Trees Road.

It always came as a surprise when people from other counties would say to me: 'You're from the city. You live in Dublin.' I spent my whole childhood playing over endless fields, hiding from Indians and damming streams with my oldest and best friend, Maurice Walsh (grandson of the writer of the same name), who lived with his grandparent in a beautiful mansion called Árd na Glaise, in Stillorgan Park. I spent much of my time sitting at the feet of the great man, and learned a great deal from him.

He was a real hard-working professional writer, with a prolific output, and a great host. There were magic nights in that house, when Scots and Kerry poets could be heard reciting their own verses, and when I had reached student age, he handed me a glass of single malt whiskey, saying: 'Always treat that with respect son. That is one of the good things of the earth.'

Maurice Walsh had his brother living with him, a dignified figure called Uncle Thade. He had fought in the Boer War, and even as a child I was aware that I was listening to a living connection with a far-gone time, when he told us of his experiences at places with romantic-sounding names like Colenso and Ladysmith. Even at an early age I realised with awe that two world wars had taken place since that time.

Maurice Walsh's faithful retainer was Tom O'Gorman, immortalised in the book *Tomasheen James: Man of No Work*. He was an eccentric creature, who had been found and taken in and given bed and board in one of the many out offices of the house. He was the general handyman and rough gardener about the place (Maurice Walsh was a wonderful gardener himself). Occasionally we used to tease him by throwing pine cones on the immaculate lawn after he had mown it. This would infuriate him, and we would get a great chase.

The climax of this was when he cornered us one day, and was moving in dangerously close, when Maurice Walsh's sister, Bridgie, who acted as his housekeeper, appeared in a doorway and screamed at Tom not to touch us. We were lucky children. What we didn't fully realise at the time, was that Tomasheen was more than a little mentally challenged. However, he lived in fear of the 'cross word' from Bridgie.

Tomasheen always sported highly polished boots, a throwback to his days of service in the British Forces. His trousers ended half way up his shins, and he always wore an apron made of sacking.

He wore his eccentric uniform on all occasions, be it travelling to Blackrock for shopping or drinking (of which he did a lot), or working in the garden. After a drinking spree, he would shout all sorts of abuse about everybody and everything about him as he made his way home.

He could be quite witty on occasion. There was another eccentric character named Harry Williams, who was also given to shouting at passers-by, and airing his philosophical and religious views. One day he encountered Tomasheen coming up from Blackrock, well filled with pints of Guinness, and told him that he believed in reincarnation. He was a snivelly kind of a little man, pale, with a hooked nose, somewhat like Mr Punch, who always wore a soft hat and longish overcoat. Tomasheen looked at him in scorn.

'Reincarnation is it? Well I'll tell ye something then: when you come back, you'll come as a parrot, and we'll throw a rug over yer cage, and there won't be an effin' word outa' ye!'

Our house, Rosemount, was one of four mansions, built by Lord Proby, on the Proby Estates, which comprised much of the surrounding lands. It was really a fitting trophy for my father, who was a multi-talented man, and justly celebrated in his day, in fact his name became well known nationally early in his career. He joined the civil service at the age of fifteen and sat the Junior Executive examination some time later.

After a wide assortment of jobs, ranging from Industry and Commerce to the Department of Education, my father ended up working at Radio Éireann (forerunner of RTÉ), where he rose to the top, as Director of Broadcasting.

When he was only nineteen, he pooled his meagre life's savings with those of two friends, Arthur Booth and Tom Collins, to found the aforementioned humorous magazine, *Dublin Opinion*. Booth was the father figure, being somewhat older than the other two. He was an extremely talented cartoonist, and one of his best drawings is to be seen on the cover of the very first edition.

Tom Collins was the literary force, writing the cleverest of humorous essays and paragraphs. My father also did a fair amount of writing. The trio had decided that after the bitterness of the Civil War, the country needed to recover its sense of humour. The motto of *Dublin Opinion* was 'Humour is the Safety Valve of the Nation'. I think they were right.

There has to be some vehicle for showing the obverse possibilities of the doings of governments. Thus, the more dictatorial politicians always view humour as something subversive. Political satirists tend to be shot under dictatorships. Certainly, my father had reason to know that not everybody had recovered a sense of humour.

On one occasion, when he was working in the Department of Education, in Marlborough Street, he was reliably tipped off that there was an unsavoury character waiting across the street to do him some bodily harm when he came out from work. He had to be helped out a back window by his boss. A nice bit of recognition for a very junior civil servant!

The first edition of the magazine didn't sell too well, and the brave trio were very disheartened, but thanks to the generous help and support of Eason's booksellers, newsagents and distributors – they got a free 'box out' (general distribution throughout the country) – the second issue sold out. They were up and running, and the magazine continued in production for forty-six years.

It is interesting to note that although the magazine was called *Dublin Opinion*, it was to be found on the table in almost every farmhouse kitchen in the country. I don't think that any publication has ever bridged the urban–rural divide so effectively.

It puzzled many people that the busy top civil servant could find time to co-produce a monthly magazine, but one of the most puzzled was Seán MacEntee, who made several efforts to raise the matter in the Dáil. My father had committed the cardinal sin of cartooning 'The Chief', as de Valera was known to the party faithful, and the irony was that my father was a 'bargain basement' voter, like myself, and sometimes actually did vote for Fianna Fáil candidates.

During McEntee's last effort to raise the matter in the Dáil, he was thwarted by James Dillon (the best orator to emerge in the new state), who constantly interrupted him, saying: 'Name the man, name the man.' Either convention or the rules of the house ruined his effort. Apparently civil servants were blessed with anonymity in the Dáil.

Mind you, my father really logged up a few major sins with the Fianna Fáil party faithful. He almost single-handedly undid the party's two efforts to abolish proportional representation. On one occasion he drew a cartoon, derived from a famous Fry's Cocoa advertisement, showing a schoolteacher standing at the head of a row of three schoolboys, arranged by height. Drawn on the blackboard were three apples, and the teacher was saying: 'Three boys, three apples. Under PR, each boy gets an apple. Under first-past-the-post, the biggest boy gets the lot.' In my view, and certainly in the view of many others, this one cartoon effectively scuppered Fianna Fáil's efforts to bring about a one-party state.

On another occasion, when Fianna Fáil was again attempting remove proportional representation, my father drew a cartoon of de Valera as Rowan Hamilton, the famous Irish mathematician who scratched his theorem on Broom Bridge lest he forget it. In the cartoon, Dev was in the same posture at the same bridge on the Grand Canal, his back to the viewer, and sporting his unmistakable hat and long black coat. Dev (a mathematician himself) had scratched on the bridge: 'FF − PR = FF^n'. Nothing could have made the issue clearer.

To my certain knowledge, my father was meticulous about never using the state's time to draw or write for *Dublin Opinion*. I well remember him rising from his desk in the GPO – which then housed Radio Éireann – on the dot of 1 p.m., and striding smartly to the magazine's office on Middle Abbey Street for an editorial conference with Tom Collins, and then looking at his watch at 1.55 p.m. and striding back again.

He was one of the bright new Turks, who really were 'professional' civil servants, and who helped with their commitment to their work to build up the new state, and who would have died rather than waste a farthing of the state's money. The big option for a good career when the new state was founded was the civil service. There were few people with names like Charlie Kelly on the boards of Irish companies, at a time when roughly five per cent of the population, most of them Protestants, owned nearly all of Irish industry.

This is not a criticism of these Protestants, who were worthy people, and left behind by the British Empire. In fact there is an old chestnut about the two Irish businessmen in a pub, and one asks the other: 'Which would you prefer doing business with, an honest Irish Catholic, or an honest Irish Protestant?' And the other answers: 'I think a Protestant, because they are more honest.'

But the new breed of 'honest Irish Catholic' finally got their revenge on my father when Fianna Fáil got back into power again, replacing John A. Costello's inter-party government. They had him shifted sideways into the job of Director of Savings, a job to which he was quite unsuited, and which almost broke the poor man's heart. He was stuck in that job until he retired. I could hear the howls of anguish from my parents' bedroom while my poor mother tried to comfort him. It was the first time I had heard a grown man cry, and the memory of it still saddens me.

Thus it may be seen that my father was a very busy man indeed. He had to meet a monthly deadline with *Dublin Opinion*, and he would frequently come home from work, eat a quick meal, and sit down at his desk or easel and work until 11 p.m. For part of every month he was not available to us. This certainly affected his relationship with me. Of course, I cannot speak for the other members of my family.

I think that he inherited something of the Victorian idea of fatherhood. You could be photographed with your babies when they were very small, but after that you didn't have to be 'hands-on'. He was never a tactile person when we were growing up, and when he kissed you, you would rub your face a good few times afterwards. But all the while, I feel quite sure that he thought he was physically close to us.

Fortunately, during the summer, when the Dáil would be in lengthy recess, the magazine deadlines would be less demanding, and we would get away for a fortnight's family holiday to a farm in Ballinglen, in Co. Wicklow.

In spite of my father's busy schedule, my parents entertained on a fair scale. It was customary at the time for people to hold 'musical evenings'. Guests would even bring their accompaniments along with them for the pianist, in the sure expectation that they would be asked to sing.

This was before the advent of delicatessen food in Ireland. Such things as 'Russian' salad were quite a novelty. This dish consisted of potato salad, mixed with diced carrots and peas, dressed with home-made mayonnaise, with beetroot around the edge of the platter. The centre-pieces on the table would be a sliced cooked ham and a couple of sliced cooked chickens, with 'bridge rolls' on the side plates, at the table's edge. These were not unlike today's rolls, which we take for granted, but somewhat more doughy. My mother would prepare a large dish of fruit salad with whipped cream to follow.

My parents didn't drink, but there were liberal supplies of wine and stout, and some whiskey, provided for the evening. There was never a lot of whiskey consumed. Stout was synonymous with the idea of a party then, and most women didn't drink.

As soon as the guests had retired into our drawing room for the rest of the evening, the young Kellys would descend on the leavings, astonished that grown-ups could be so absent-minded as to leave so much unconsumed. I remember filling my face with delicious forbidden fruits.

My mother would admonish us not to fall on the food, but invariably we did, and for some reason or other, she never remarked on its disappearance. I think that she was quietly amused.

While the performances were taking place, the younger Kellys would run upstairs in their pyjamas to listen at the drawing room door to 'Pale Hands I Loved, Beside The Shalimar', or 'Lindenlea'.

Then there was the delicious terror as a guest came to the door, on the way to the bathroom, and we would flee upstairs, like squirrels up a tree, and lie 'doggo' until the guest had gone back into the room again. My sisters would then go up to my parents' bedroom, and try on the fur coats of my mother's friends, and totter around in my mother's high heels, talking 'guest speak', saying things like: 'Kathleen, you're great, do you know that? Such a large family and such a big house, I don't know how you manage it.'

Once I was caught short in the hall as the drawing room door opened, and I ran behind the coat stand and climbed in among the hanging coats, clinging for dear life to the central pod, while the guest frisked all the coats, and unknowingly, me as well, for his elusive cigarettes, and after what seemed like an age, found his own coat, and withdrawing the cigarettes with a grunt, re-entered the room. I emerged even skinnier from that coat stand.

There were pictures hung on both sides of the fourth and highest level of the staircase at the top of our house, and these formed a natural gallery. Sometimes my father would take his guests to see the pictures during one of these gala evenings. On this particular evening, the main centre hanging light had given up the ghost. There was always difficulty replacing it, as this required the placing of a large and wide plank from banister to banister to reach it.

I had been listening at the drawing room door, and as it opened I fled upstairs in my pyjamas, right to the top of the house, around the end of the banisters, and threw myself flat in the shadows on the bare floorboards of the 'gallery', in against the wall. My father and his guests trooped upstairs to look at the pictures. Fortunately I was concealed in the gloom. I lay terrified, like a trapped hare, my breathing rapid and shallow to avoid detection. They seemed to discuss the pictures forever, and then slowly returned downstairs. It was the nearest I ever came to being a stain on the floor.

There were also many grand evenings, when musicians who were guests with the Symphony Orchestra, played their violins passionately, to the accompaniment of some renowned pianist, all as guests of the Director of Radio Éireann. In this way it was a privileged upbringing for us all. To this day, I hear famous names in music, literature and art, and find myself saying casually: 'O yes, he was a friend of my father's', or 'She sang in our house one time'.

There were let downs, too. The late Canon Sydney McEwan had been a guest in our house, and when he appeared in Dublin a second time, my mother invited him for an evening, and a truly splendid repast was prepared. But he never turned up. There are some performers who have scant respect for true and sincere hospitality, and in our experience, he was one of them.

My mother was a 'goodish' but flustered cook. We were once visited by Archbishop Hurley, of Durban, who at forty-four, was the youngest archbishop in the world. Everything had been prepared for dinner in the kitchen, including an exotic soup, made to a new recipe, over which my mother had taken immense trouble, and which only remained to be strained into another pot. The straining began, but unfortunately she omitted to put a pot in the sink to catch the soup. It all went down the plughole, to my mother's consternation. In desperation, tinned soup was chucked into a pot and rapidly heated.

Dinner proceeded, with my mother scarlet-faced at the top of the table as the soup was consumed. Her own courses followed, succulent and beautifully presented. When dinner was over, the Archbishop complimented my mother on the soup, which he said was the high point of the whole meal.

My parents allowed us to keep open house, entertaining our friends, mainly in the kitchen. You would never know who you might meet there after a dance in Anglesea Lawn Tennis Club or Old Belvedere Rugby Club, popular venues at the time. My mother would leave the remains of Saturday's roast for us to make sandwiches.

I often had to step over the long legs of Tony O'Reilly, now Sir Anthony O'Reilly, and I know that he remembers, because he once bypassed all the bigwigs at the Galway Oyster Festival to say hello, and to tell me that he would never forget my mother's kitchen.

Of course there was method in my mother's madness. Both she and my father knew that their family were safely at home when they heard the laughter coming from the kitchen.

Rosemount, Avoca Avenue, was a lovely place to grow up in. There was a wonderfully dense shrubbery for us to dodge dart-blowing pygmies and a huge sycamore tree to climb. Sometimes my brother and sister (the twins) and I used to spend our pocket money on three packets of wine gums each and climb the tree on a summer's evening.

The convent across the road was a training college for women primary school teachers, who had to be back in their quarters by 10 p.m. Their amorous leave-takings of their boyfriends took place in our shrubbery, and some evenings we used to have to sit in silence up the tree, watching the canoodling. It was most instructive, if moderate by modern standards. When we descended, stiff from being tree-bound for so long, we felt like swollen balls of glycerine. Just you try eating three packets of wine gums at the one sitting!

My father was intensely proud of his front lawn, which looked like a great white carpet when the snow fell. Snow was forecast and he was looking forward to the great spectacle. However, my brother was going through a phase of finding his identity by autographing everything he possessed.

The snow fell thickly, and my father rose early in the day in pleasant anticipation of the glorious spectacle. He opened his bedroom curtains to see my brother's name written the entire length of the lawn. The phantom had struck! If I remember correctly, he took it rather well.

I have the happiest memories of playing in that garden. On dark winter evenings, my brother and a friend of his, who was a neighbour, would lie in wait for the crowds making their way up Avoca Avenue from the Regent Cinema and the pubs in Blackrock. They were a fairly tough crowd, soldiers home on leave, who had money to spend on drink, and the denizens of the damp cottages.

My brother and his accomplice would have placed dog's dirt strategically on the pavement, with a lighted cigarette butt on top. We would run behind our high hedge and await developments. In all these crowds there is a natural leader, who chooses the songs and leads the dance.

It was common for people to sing-songs on their way home from the pubs in those days, and the leader would invariably spot the cigarette butt, and as people do, he just couldn't resist stamping it out. He would dance out to the tempo of the song, and execute a massive and spectacular ski slide on the dog shite, accompanied by a series of blasphemies sufficient to turn the blue night white. Ah, childhood joys!

4

A Formidable Woman

My mother had a wonderful mind, but was a victim of the terrible system whereby a woman had to give up her job once she was married. She was extremely well read, and in my adolescence we used to discuss books endlessly.

She had a wide knowledge of history and poetry, and had read most of the great novelists. My father used to say to me when I was bored and looking for something to do: 'Why don't you go and read a good book?' I well remember thinking: 'Not for you I bloody won't!'

Actually my father wasn't really very well read. He seemed to have convinced himself that he was by promoting the virtues of good literature to others. I think he picked up most of his references from my mother, and like me, having a 'trivial pursuit' mind, could sound better read than he was.

Many years later, when I was a married man, with a household of children, he confessed to me that he wasn't really very well read, and this led to a strange relationship between us, whereby I would feed him all the formative books by authors like W. Somerset Maugham, Aldous Huxley, Evelyn Waugh, Graham Greene, John Steinbeck and Sinclair Lewis, and he would guzzle them gratefully. It wasn't that my father had read none of these authors. He would have read some of them, but just an early work here and there.

I think the truth was that, with his Atlas-like workload, there had never been time for him to read until he retired from the civil service. Like many of his generation, he had read all of Charles Dickens in his youth, or indeed, as was common then, had it read to him as well. When he died, he left me the entire *Dublin Opinion* archive, and all of his books, and I find it quite moving when I open one of them, now and then, to find 'Love from Frank to Dad' written in the flyleaf.

My mother's life was centred on her six children, and she dreaded the day when we would be grown and gone, and she would face a terrible vacuum. I know this, because she frequently told me so. I came into the kitchen one day, and she was sitting, crying, listening to a song which contained the words 'and the children are children no more'.

Her powerful intellect could tolerate a fairly rough-edged joke, provided that it was really funny, and although she was a deeply spiritual catholic, she detested prudery. Once she held a 'girls evening' for all her circle of friends to show them the patterns for the bride's and bridesmaids' dresses for my sister's forthcoming wedding.

Subsequently an emissary was sent to tell her that the consensus of all her friends was that the bridesmaids' dresses were too low in the front. The message that she sent back was that, if they thought that, then perhaps they had better not come. They all came, and the subject was never mentioned again.

She was before her time in being very impatient with the presumptuous behaviour of many of the Catholic clergy, which was common at that time. There was much grovelling on the part of the laity, and priests might call to our house without warning, and if a tasty meal was provided and consumed without any sign of appreciation and was merely taken for granted as 'the little woman's work', the cleric would leave the house with a sore fleabite in his ear.

Once my parents took a priest for a meal in the restaurant at Dublin Airport, which was the height of style at the time, and he ordered lobster, which was the most expensive dish on the menu. It duly arrived, and halfway through consuming it, he lit up a cigarette, smoked it and stubbed it out on the lobster. My mother came home bristling. It didn't matter who you were, you were never off the hook with my mother when it came to ordinary good manners. He never crossed our door again.

She had quite an offbeat sense of humour from time to time. When Blackrock Parish church was undergoing reconstruction, there was a huge section of masonry hanging high in mid-air in a loop of chain. For some reason or another the rear door of the church had been left open, and my mother walked unthinkingly under this potentially highly dangerous hazard, and a chivalrous man ran after her, warning her of the danger, but this heavy little fair woman smiled vaguely, saying: 'Thank you so much, but I prefer to live dangerously.' She was a great fan of James Thurber – the famous American author, journalist and cartoonist – and not uninfluenced by his style of humour.

Much of her time was spent mooning around our large basement kitchen on days when she would be depressed, and wondering where her life was going, as we all grew rapidly and began to go our separate ways, but her sense of humour could usually take her out of a trough if you chose the right opportunity to make her laugh.

When there was rousing music on the radio during my teens, I used to grab her and waltz her around the flagged kitchen. 'Come Mother,' I would say, 'let us dance the Katuca,' and in spite of her protestations, away we would go in a wild dance while she protested vociferously, but to no avail, eventually dissolving into helpless laughter.

My father moved at great speed through life, and my mother was hard-put to keep up with him. She was always giving out to him for walking too fast for her. He was a smart dresser, wearing an Anthony Eden hat and a black swing coat, tailor-made suits, hand-made shirts and shoes, and the smartest of ties. His shoes were steel-tipped, and we could always hear the smack of his heels

37

on the pavement as he strode up Avoca Avenue from Blackrock train station on the way home from work.

Between his being Director of Radio Éireann and a co-founder of *Dublin Opinion*, my parents had a pretty hectic social life. I still don't know how my father managed to fit all this in with his work. My poor mother, who was very short of stature, and always overweight, definitely felt the strain. He had been a masher (dance hall glamour boy) in his day, and still fancied himself on the ballroom floor.

Invariably he would team up with someone's glamorous wife, and they would dance the night away. My poor little mother would hardly get a look in. God bless her, she couldn't put one foot in front of the other. On one occasion, they had been to a gala dance in the Gresham Hotel, and they were making their way to a taxi rank, while my father complained about the terrible pains in his calves, which had developed from the unaccustomed dancing.

So bad was the pain, that he had to take off his shoes and walk in his socks. My mother turned on him in fury, saying: 'Well hell slap it into you. You've spent the whole night dancing with that hussy.' Her mother was from Cavan, and she had inherited a raft of country sayings, which only emerged from her psyche when she was enraged.

Also, she had some sayings that were not born out of anger, and were highly descriptive. One was: 'As quick as a cock on a raspberry.' Now, if you have ever watched a free-range cockerel swoop on a wild raspberry behind a cow house, you will know what that means, but you would want to be quick. It is almost faster than the eye can see.

My father was always the centre of attention, and my mother would find herself at the edge of the throng which would gather around him, waiting for his next bon mot, and he wouldn't disappoint them. He was extremely witty. Really, what attracted them was the *Dublin Opinion* connection. Because the magazine contained so much witty material, they expected the same on the hoof, and he delivered. Frequently, when they returned from some soirée, my mother would be in very bad humour, with her face as red as a turkey cock's.

Invariably, he was quite oblivious to the wrongs he perpetrated on her. It was as though he suffered from an incurable blindness. He loved her, and would never have willingly hurt her, and she loved him, although he drove her crazy most of the time. When she died, he said to me: 'You see Frank, it's the end of such a long conversation.' That wasn't the kind of thing you could have said about a truly unhappy marriage.

5

Rural Idyll

My parents acquired a forestry cottage by tender at Rednagh Hill, Aughrim, Co. Wicklow. It was actually on a couple of acres, cut out of the forest, and bordered by a line of impressive cypress trees. The tendering process depended on the sense of responsibility of the applicants, because you couldn't light bonfires on the land, for obvious reasons, and anyone occupying such a dwelling would have to have the interests of the Forestry Department at heart.

The cottage came at a time in the life of the family when people were setting out on their careers, or involved in intensive studies at university, and thus was really underused by the family, except for picnics for groups of their friends, but my father and mother got good use out of it themselves.

It really was an idyllic setting, five hundred feet above the village, and seven hundred and fifty feet above sea level. I always had dreams of using it, but I acquired such a large family with such rapidity that something always got in the way of our getting there when the children were small, and our annual trip to West Cork or the West of Ireland were all we could manage. Eventually, the last of my sisters to marry was given it by the family after the deaths of my parents, and she sold it for reasons of her own.

However, the times I did spend there, further imbued me with an undying love of that part of the country, which had been born during our early post-war holidays in nearby Ballinglen House.

This was a Georgian country mansion farmhouse, owned by our good friends, Ned and Nora Boyd, where we went for our annual summer holidays as children. Their hospitality was well beyond the contract; they treated us with a warmth and friendship, which affected all of us deeply. They had four children, Campbell, Betty, Harry and Joan, who quickly became our friends.

We had the run of their huge farm, and I remember every inch of it. It was 'mixed' farming: acres of cereal crops, a large herd of cattle, a big flock of sheep, and hundreds of free-range fowl, to which we used to give false-alarm feeding calls, and bring them running to us in their legions. Poor Mrs Boyd used to scold us for doing this, quite rightly, but the temptation was always too great. Children love a sense of power.

Ned Boyd had a stallion, named Danno, which used to service all the mares in the surrounding countryside, and there was always a great air of excitement when the day arrived for the servicing.

The visiting farmer would be entertained with bottles of stout in the kitchen, and then the main event would commence.

We would do anything to conceal ourselves, where we might watch the majestic sight of the stallion mounting the mare. Once, we were concealed in a granary, which was at the top of a steep flight of granite steps. You could see under the door from where we lay on our bellies on the grain, each of us having taken the husks off a goodly pile to eat during the performance.

It had only commenced, when some form of telepathy told Ned Boyd that we were in our grandstand position. Proceedings were halted, and we were banished from our cosy nest. Bitter disappointment.

The Boyds also had a great black bull, a huge and truly dangerous fellow, named Bally Ram Michael, who was kept on his own in the more remote fields. He had the look of a Spanish fighting bull about him, and even to see him in the distance was thrilling. One dark night, before rural electrification, when there would be no light anywhere on the skyline, and you could have cut the darkness with a knife, Nora Boyd had occasion to go out the front door. Instantly, some primeval instinct told her that she was in mortal danger. She stepped back inside the door, closing it quietly, as the bull charged towards it, skidding to a halt, puzzled that his quarry had disappeared.

In those days, there was a railway line from Woodenbridge all the way to Ballinglen. When one arrived on the train, the station master, who kept beautiful flower beds on his platform, used to don his CIÉ hat, put on his jacket, and greet all the passengers personally as they got off the train.

There was no turntable at Ballinglen, and the train had to reverse all the way back to Woodenbridge. When I had a family of my own, I made a nostalgic pilgrimage back to the territory which had provided such happiness for us all. My eyes filled with tears when I beheld a mature tree growing in the middle of the space which had been occupied by the railway line.

Every morning, Ned Boyd would take the milk churns to the station on a flat cart pulled by a glorious grey horse, named Cash. If you were late for the trip, there was no stopping Ned. He would shout 'hup chaps' and away he would go. If you were late you had to hop up on the cart while it was in motion. I well remember charging across the big main front field, climbing a stile about a quarter of a mile along the route, and intercepting the cart with a great sense of triumph.

When we arrived for our holiday, we would be met by the horse and trap at Ballinglen station, and the rumble of the wheels on the unmetalled road was matched in magic only by the huge musculature of the horse's rump, especially when he answered a call of nature in transit.

Ned Boyd was my first hero, and I was eight years of age when he died. This was my first real consciousness of death. We went to his funeral in Preban Church of Ireland Church, and stood outside in the rain during the service. At this time, Catholic Church rules forbade attendance at services of other denominations under pain of excommunication. I knew that this rule was wrong, just plainly wrong, although I was only eight. I count this as my first moral certainty. I had to stand outside in the rain, while others prayed for the soul of my hero inside in the church. It was a time of extreme legalism in the Catholic Church, and we are the better for its passing.

A great treat was a trip to Aughrim, when petrol had returned to Ireland, and the journey to Ballinglen was made in our family car. There we would visit Major Con McSwiney and his wife, Maura, who lived in the gate lodge of the Aughrim mill. We would be allowed to swim in the millrace, which seemed like a great waterway to me then, but now looks diminutive when I pass.

'The Major', as he was known, had been for many years the schoolteacher in Aughrim. He was a Corkman and a Gaelic scholar, and had been in the British Army during the First World War. During the war, he had been Acting Governor of Cyprus for a time. He had also been Private Secretary to John Redmond, of the Irish Parliamentary Party. I found his talk fascinating, and would sit at his feet, spellbound. I only realised that the affection was reciprocated, when, after he died, I found that he left me three histories of Ireland, which had belonged to Redmond, one of which is autographed by the great man.

6

Talented Child Syndrome

When I was very small I was brought to see Fred Astaire and Ginger Rogers in a black and white movie, in which Fred did a dance routine on the floor, tables and chairs, which he punctuated with bangers, and I was so taken with this that I did the same, without the bangers, on our own kitchen tables and chairs to music from the radio. From that moment my parents decided that I was a born performer. Nobody had decided just what kind of a performer, but I was destined to be one. I had a good singing voice – at least, I was always being asked to sing, so there must have been some truth in it.

When I went to primary school in Willow Park, it was soon discovered that I had 'a voice', and was earmarked for the leading roles in the school operettas. It was indeed a very good soprano voice, but I thought nothing of it, and didn't welcome the attention which it drew to me.

I began piano lessons, and quite enjoyed them. On my seventh birthday, which occurred on 28 December 1945, I rose from my bed, bursting with excitement at the prospect of receiving my present. Being the date it was, my father was on leave from work, and I ran downstairs to be confronted by my parents, both clad in their dressing gowns. My father had a huge grin on his face, and both hands behind his back. When he brought them to the front, in his right hand was a minute violin case.

'Go on son,' he said, 'take it, and open it.' My heart had sunk to my bowels. Whatever else I might have wanted, I didn't want a violin.

I took it and opened it, and inside was a small dark, honey-coloured violin, nestling in egg-yoke yellow, furry lining. 'Well son,' he said, 'isn't it beautiful? That's the bow there. Clipped to the lid. Go on, lift it out.'

I did as I was bade, gingerly, and with feelings of the deepest disappointment. This was going to be the first, and probably the most demanding acting job of my life. I told my father that I thought it was beautiful, the most beautiful thing I had ever seen. I lied my face off, unable to bring myself to hurt his feelings, because I knew that he loved me, and thought he was giving me a great present. But remember, I was only seven, and had no toy to play with. You can play a violin, but you can't play 'with' a violin. By the way, my piano lessons were discontinued when I returned to school after the Christmas holidays. This was quite a pity, because I like the piano, and still enjoy messing around on it to this day, so much so that I think I might have become a pretty competent pianist. But this was not to be.

At the tender age of nine, no less, I was seconded to play the female roles in the senior Blackrock College Gilbert and Sullivan production, as well as the Willow Park one. By this time I had acquired a maestro, a Polish refugee violinist who had joined the newly-formed Radio Éireann Symphony Orchestra, and become a friend of my father's.

This man lived with his aged parents in a flat on Dublin's Baggot Street, on the top floor. There was a thick steel plate on the back of the specially-hung door of their flat, in readiness for 'the knock in the night'. The mother was the typical dumpy Polish peasant woman you will see in any travel book, but the father was a tall, stooped figure, who always wore his little yarmulke in the house, and was almost certainly Jewish, although this was hotly denied by the maestro and his mother. My maestro was born in Odessa, and was a fervent Roman Catholic, as was his mother.

They each had a tremendous devotion to the Blessed Virgin, and particularly to the Polish 'Our Lady Of Czestachova', whose protection they both invoked constantly. They had fled throughout Europe ahead of the Nazis, and I always felt that the yarmulke was the cause of their difficulties.

It only dawned on me after some years of his tuition that it must have been very reassuring for my maestro to have had such a close friendship with the head honcho of Radio Éireann after fleeing ahead of the Nazis throughout the war.

His father had been a lawyer, although what particular kind I do not know. How do you keep a law practice going if you are constantly on the move? When he died, his widow told me that it was important that they keep his death a close secret, 'because people are very dishonest, you know, and if they knew he was dead they would cease to do business with him'. This always puzzled me.

I had to go on the bus into town, to Baggot Street, for my lessons, climb the four flights of steps to the flat, and knock repeatedly on the door before it was opened. There would be a screech of 'who is thees?' from inside, and I would have to declare my identity. Then the door would be opened just a crack, still on the chain. When it was finally opened by the old woman, I stepped straight into middle Europe. There were huge sausages hanging from the ceiling, and she would reach out for a sharp knife and cut a hunk for me and thrust it into my hand.

'Eat,' she would say. 'Ees very good for little boy! In Poland little boys are liking this sausage very much. Eat! Ees good, very very good.' And I would have to chew an appalling concoction of gristle, garlic and unknown spices, which made my eyes water.

Another delicacy was a substance like sweet gritty putty, flavoured with almonds. I later learned that this was halva. But on the whole I would have settled for a bar of chocolate.

When you add together two major roles in the school operettas, mandatory violin practice and rugby, there was little time for academic study. I had soon fallen far behind, but this was excused on the grounds that I was 'artistic'. This was said pityingly, and in hushed tones, not unlike the way people say 'autistic'.

References to my appearances in the school productions were frequently made by my bogmen teachers, and my colleagues would then feel free to call me by the name of my current female role in the recreation ground. This made me quite aggressive. If I was going to have to fight for respect, then that was it in playground logic. After I had bloodied a few noses, people avoided calling me funny names.

There was always a high standard of debate in our home. Conversation at mealtimes ranged widely. It might seem unlikely that such a highly-strung and slightly pedantic individual as my father would encourage debate, but now I think that conversation, no matter how contentious, was his literature.

This gave all the Kellys a marked ability to speak up for themselves, clearly and distinctly, an ability which was not always welcomed by our rural teachers.

I can't speak for my sisters' school, but many of our teachers were teachers by default. They had either been invalided home from the missions, or had never been let do the missionary work, for which they had joined the Holy Ghost Order, and as priests, they must have found it very frustrating. The lay teachers, with some exceptions, seemed to be more comfortable vocationally, if somewhat eccentric. But there was a breed which came with a big collective chip on their shoulder about spoiled little brats from the east coast.

This manifested itself in exhortations to 'speak yer native tongue', which of course was complete nonsense. Where in God's name would we hear people speaking Irish in Leinster? The tongue you are born into is your native tongue. But bogmen ruled supreme in those days, unhindered by their more enlightened colleagues, and de Valera's 'crossroads logic' had to be put into practice.

Much of their arrogance was paid for by 'inevadible' income tax, which was deducted at source to pay for the myth that the Gaeltacht was thriving.

Interesting to note that the splendid gaelschoileanna which have sprung up along the east coast were the brainchildren of intelligent people with a true love of Irish, but not just that, a true love of education as well. It took people power to teach governments how to go about it, and fair play to them.

The presentation to me of the violin by my father when I was seven set the tone for our relationship until I was in my mid-thirties. What a waste of so many years. You see, what he was doing was living out his fantasy of being a concert violinist through me. Had I told him that I had won the hundred metres sprint in the Olympic Games, he would have raised his eyebrows and asked with a patient smile: 'Yes, but did you do your violin practice?' And yes, he was a bit of a pedant. If you said to him: 'Daddy, I got a place on the team, and I wasn't even meant to,' he would say quietly: 'Intended to.'

Thus, I developed a habit of avoiding his company as much as I could. He loved me. I knew that, but he just couldn't show it, and because I used so much subterfuge to avoid him and my violin practice, I began to like him less and less. I felt very guilty about this, because your religion told you to love your parents, and while I was passionately devoted to my mother, as the years rolled by I began to develop a sense of total indifference towards my father.

One Sunday my maestro was invited to lunch at our house, and during the meal it dawned on my father that it would be possible to combine Sunday lunch with my violin lesson. What a brilliant idea! First I would have my lesson at twelve noon, and that would be followed by lunch. And so that was to be it for many months at a time.

My lovely Sunday mornings hanging out with my friends were gone, and Sunday lunches were punctuated by singularly unfunny Central European jokes, as my father and my teacher slapped their thighs in ecstatic amusement, while the family stared at them uneasily.

What my mother must have thought of all this I can only imagine. She can't have liked having this man at her table every

Sunday, but her husband would have his way. I know one thing: he wouldn't have had the slightest idea that he was discommoding anybody. The strange thing was that I had a definite talent for the violin.

At an early stage I was laying quite a sophisticated repertoire for my age: Viotti, Accolay's 'Concerto', 'Méditation' from Massenet's *Thaïs*, and 'Ballade et Polonaise' by Henri Vieuxtemps.

All the extra-curricular activities impacted rather badly on any chance I had of academic achievement. I was the only boy in my year in Willow Park who failed the primary certificate. Again, my musical talent was brought out as an excuse: 'He gives so much pleasure with the music that we can't expect too much.' But they kept me back a year (with the consent of my parents), and I was separated from all my friends, whose birthday parties I had gone to, and with whom I had been at convent school.

I was now a year older than my classmates, and I found this highly embarrassing. Meanwhile the violin torture continued, with more intensity really, as the gap between my father and me widened. I was now terrified by the hatred I was beginning to feel for my father. I overcame this fear to a degree by the realisation that there was much written about filial duty in the Old Testament, and my uneducated mind was able to settle for that. I would be dutiful, and that would count as love.

I was once guilty of behaviour for which I would now send any child for whom I was responsible to a psychologist for analysis. When I was growing up we were allowed to have air pistols and rifles, and although they were highly dangerous, they were great fun. I had a Diana air pistol, and one day as I prepared to practise my violin, I spied the pistol out of the corner of my eye.

I loaded it and took a test shot, at my music sheet. My God, the frisson when the pellet went through a quaver! I reloaded and fired again, and then again and again until the music was in flitters. I don't recall what happened after that. Perhaps I had a spare copy, or more likely, I told some outrageous lie to explain its disappearance.

I succeeded in failing the intermediate certificate in two successive years, much to my humiliation. Each day I was terrified of going into school, because I had little comprehension of many of my subjects, particularly maths and Irish. As I look back now, I can see that much of my giddiness in class was really a defence. It masked the terror I felt of being exposed as being quite ignorant of the very basic elements of many of my subjects.

I naturally gravitated towards the role of class clown. It seemed that I had an in-built capacity for making people laugh. This was considered highly subversive, more by the bogmen than by anybody else. It is interesting to note that there were certain priests who seemed to be able to take people's ability to be funny in their stride, and just get on with teaching, unperturbed by the odd laugh.

What is it about humour which produces such paranoia in people, and leads them to treat it as some sort of commodity? I was once asked by a captain of industry to add some humour to his annual company report, as he always felt that it was a bit dull. Well it was dull, just about as dull as its author. I declined the commission, explaining that it was quite impossible to supply someone with a sense of humour.

What people don't seem to realise is that humour is basically irony. It is truly ironic that the fat man striding along, full of self-importance, should suddenly slip on a banana skin and land on his backside. This irony permeates all good new alternative comedy if you listen closely.

The shame and sense of inferiority produced by my double fault in the Inter Cert stakes made me begin to take stock of my position. Here I was, star of all the school shows, fairly good at sport, but left far behind academically. I would have to get my act together. But how? No one was going to help me. I would just have to do it on my own.

The bright idea dawned on my father that I should be sent to Paris to further my musical studies. This produced a reaction of complete terror in me. I was to be taken away from my friends and family, and my beloved mother, to a place about which I knew nothing. My mother heard me sobbing in my room, and for once confronted my father and completely down-faced him. We heard no more about Paris after that. There must have been one hell of a row.

I did a little personal audit, and realised that I must confront my father and give up the violin. The school shows would have to go as well, whatever the reaction. I would have to grow up and fight for myself. No more 'Mr Nice Guy'!

Firstly, my father. When I told him, he just stared into space, saying nothing for a while. He didn't put up much resistance. I think that something in my demeanour told him that there was no point in fighting. It was a watershed moment between us.

Then there was the school. When I told the very kind and nice priest who directed the shows that I was giving up, he was gobsmacked. 'But you can't do that after all the musical training we have given you!'

I had to explain that I had brought my musical education with me, having had my own personal maestro for ten years. After all, the Gilbert and Sullivan songs were taught to us by ear; we didn't work from the written music. A huge amount of my educational time had been taken from me for the glory of the school, and if I was going to do anything with myself, I had better start now. I didn't just suspect that I had been exploited. I knew that I had.

In spite of my father's expectations for me on the world concert circuit (God save us!), he began to consider the option of having me apprenticed to a printing house. My father would have had good connections, having had *Dublin Opinion* printed there for many years.

7

Shivering Objects of Desire

During the summer school holidays I went to Blackrock sea baths every morning, once I had reached puberty. The entrance fee was three pence for children, and when we were teenagers, if I remember rightly, it was nine pence. We were all on friendly terms with the attendants, and I think our core group was very welcome as their clientele, because we had great commitment to competitive swimming and springboard and platform diving, and this would have created an ethos of good behaviour.

It was a great way to spend your summer. We even went there in wet weather. Of course, the girls were a big attraction too. Most of us fell in or out of love about every three weeks. Of course, there was always the unattainable shivering nymphet, with whom everyone was in love all the time. The other girls didn't seem to mind this, as she posed no real threat. She was disinterested in our mute and adoring glances, or spoken for. It was rather like a married man being deeply in love with Halle Berry, with the full and contented knowledge of his wife.

Order was maintained by Jack McCann, assisted by Kit Cannon. They didn't countenance any wild or dangerous behaviour, but succeeded in teaching us genuine respect for authority. There would be few supervisors who would do so much unpaid parenting today.

Competition between the various swimming clubs was intense. The clubs based at Blackrock Baths were Young Leinster, Sandycove Swimming Club and Pembroke, and we were visited by North Dublin Swimming Club, Clontarf Otter and Bray Cove. Frequently there were water polo matches in the evenings, and there can hardly be a tougher sport.

One season there was a B. Special – a Northern Ireland Army auxiliary – playing centre forward for Bangor Swimming Club, who had had a tangle with a Sandycove centre forward, and we all felt that he had fouled our man repeatedly, undetected by the referee. We were staunchly supportive of our player, and very angry indeed. There was to be no retribution, because there was no other fixture in the season when the two teams would meet. It was all very frustrating.

The following season the two teams faced each other again. Everyone had forgotten the actual details of what had occurred between our man and theirs the previous season. The referee blew his whistle and threw the ball into the centre of the pool for the two centre forwards to compete for possession. The two players reached the ball at the same time, but whereas their man scooped the ball into his hand, ours never even tried to touch it, and put his fist into the other player's jaw. Their man was left floating in the water like a deflated balloon. The Sandycove man was immediately sent to the boxes. We cheered him mightily. The revenge was oh so sweet. Even more, it had been exacted on a B. Special!

These matches provided us with a chance to chase girls in the evenings, which was a real bonus. There were heroes, young men who were fit before the term was invented, such as the Kavanagh brothers, Paddy (Irish Rugby international and Irish hundred metres swimming champion), Ronnie (leader of the Irish Rugby forward pack for many years), Gene (rugby player of renown and champion swimmer), Danno O'Brien (diver and father of the current telephone mogul, Denis O'Brien), Joe Keegan (of Goggins

Pub, in Monkstown), Mat Feddis, and then members of a slightly younger generation, Leo Keegan, Val Demery and Billy Morrison.

Most of the above doubled as divers, and when the swimming galas came along, they gave great displays of nerve in formation diving. One breathtaking feat, in the comedy display, was diving in succession and catching each other's feet, and then detaching before they hit the water.

Leo Keegan dived through a flaming hoop from the ten metre board, and Billy Morrison and Val Demery were two of the best exponents of the swan dive I have ever seen.

Sometimes there were exotic visitors, like Peter Heatley of Highgate Diving Club in England. He was a true master of the art of high board diving. His special exhibition dive was a triple pike dive from the ten metre board. I have never heard of anyone else touching their toes three times in the air over a distance of ten metres, and then making a textbook entrance into the water. He was a true superman to us.

One summer we were visited by an Israeli men's diving team, who kissed each other on the cheek as a sign of approval after a particularly successful dive. We had never seen men kissing each other before, and were more than a little embarrassed.

But the king of the baths was Eddie Heron, who had taken part in the springboard diving event in the Olympic Games. Everyone held him in great awe. He was also a renowned platform diver, and I always thought that he never got the national recognition which he deserved. The facilities which he required materialised much later. Eddie dived until he reached a mature age, and right to the end there was no one to touch him.

I always aspired to being a champion springboard diver, but never quite made it, apart from a few minor junior titles, but there was nothing I enjoyed more than training on the board. It made for great summer memories.

One year, just before the end of the summer term, when I was in secondary school, I was approached by the Dayboys' Dean Of Studies and asked whether I would be interested in the organisation of a Blackrock College Swimming Club. I replied that I was already a member of Young Leinster Swimming Club, and that I was going to join Sandycove Swimming Cub as a matter of course.

It was then pointed out to me that there was a certain amount of 'mixed bathing' taking place in Blackrock Baths, and the club would be a means of eradicating this wanton behaviour. I couldn't believe my ears. My home was a most liberal one when it came to such issues, and my parents would have heartily approved of their children mixing happily with members of the opposite sex.

The priest was somewhat taken aback by my forceful assertion that I saw no harm in mixed bathing whatsoever. I said that I had absolutely no intention of changing my club allegiances, and that there was no chance that I would join the Blackrock Swimming Club. He was most displeased with this, but there was nothing he could do about it. I had the impression that I had confirmed his opinion of me as a 'smart alec'.

When the swimming season began, he had recruited quite a large membership, and there was a priestly presence at races. A lay brother of the order used to parade along outside the boxes in the men's changing area, saying 'Cover yer asses boys! Cover yer asses!' Apparently in his unhealthy mind there were endless vistas of opportunities for sinning, for healthy young men, naked in each others' presence.

The following season, for some reason, the club just lost energy and died out, and I was secretly very pleased. I felt that this interference in our summer social life was quite unnecessary and an unwarranted trespass.

Coming as we did from the eastern seaboard, we lived in a poly-faith environment. In our district, there were Church of Ireland, Plymouth Brethren, Jewish, and children of heaven knows what other faiths. Friendships were formed among the children in their innocent, natural way. You knew that someone was of a faith other than yours, and it made little difference. It certainly hadn't much to do with how good a roller skater you were, or whether you could cycle with your hands off the handlebars. Mind you, there was a certain curiosity and mystery, but little if any discussion of differences in faiths.

By the time we were taken aside in school and told not to mix with Protestants, it was just too late. I had friends with names like Máire, Prudence, Wendy, Jane, Aideen, Nuala, Norman, and Nigel. My soul was already headed for damnation. Protestant girls seemed to have longer and browner legs than Catholic ones. Maybe the pure Norman blood had not yet been diluted by the new red-haired and freckled state. By God they had sex appeal! Mind you, the term 'sex appeal' hadn't been invented yet. Hollywood had yet to come up with it.

Any physical encounters with a young maiden at a dance were swiftly discouraged; you were told that she was an 'occasion of sin', and that you must studiously avoid her in the future, under pain of losing your immortal soul. Thus, someone's bewildered and lovely little daughter, who may not have been fully aware of what was happening to her, was further bewildered by being completely shunned by a boyfriend.

Surely the best penance a confessor could have handed out was an obligation to present one's self to the girl, with an apology for the transgression and a promise that it wouldn't happen again. I think that the shock of this would have proved itself to be a better de-tumescent than mere abstinence from her company. It's no wonder that this regime produced a generation of young men who couldn't go to a dance without getting footless first to give them enough Dutch courage to make overtures to girls.

I mitched off from many school retreats in my day, but when I was fifteen I attended one, which formed a faith in me which has remained ever since. A Redemptorist priest was giving the sermon, and he said something which was quite revolutionary for that time, which was, 'Never be put off your faith by a silly priest.'

Now in those days for a priest to say such a thing as 'silly priest' was quite unthinkable, and there and then it brought the realisation to me that your faith is your own property, not something to be dispensed to you on a Monday, and withdrawn on a Friday.

Thus, during the controversy on birth control, and many of the pronouncements of Pope John Paul II, and hasty, sometimes multiple canonisations, I have reminded myself that nothing is going to alter my core faith. I was given it, and haven't chosen to reject it, but to try and hold on to it.

Mind you, I found that I have this in common with many secular clergy, who have to soldier on at ground level, whatever the current pronouncement from Rome, be it the rubbishing of years and years of ecumenism by the then Cardinal Ratzinger, or the canonisation of a large number of Chinese people out of the blue, by Pope John Paul II, which is so relevant to our daily lives. Were we expected to come to the astonishing conclusion that Chinese people can be holy too?

Anyone who makes the accusation of 'à la carte Catholicism' had better be sure that he or she has absolutely no doubts, and knows that many saints may have had doubts, but probably a fair dash of humility as well.

On one occasion I was summoned to the office of the Dean of Dayboys, and informed that it had come to the attention of the College that I and some other offenders were fraternising with girls on our way home each day. What would my mother think if she knew?

I was very proud to be able to say with assurance that the best way of finding out would be to phone my mother, who was sure to be at home at that time, and ask her. I was shown to the door in silence. There was a total inability in Blackrock College to cope with sexuality, and a total abdication of the responsibility to educate boys to interact properly with their female opposite numbers. If you hadn't a stable home background, with good liberal parents, you were definitely going to have a problem.

8

The Great Escape Bid

I had become increasingly embarrassed at the year's age difference between myself and my classmates. At home, I was the youngest of six children, and I had watched them all make their various mistakes, and had learned from them.

My mother never knew quite what I was up to, and this certainly was a good thing. I was quite streetwise, and spoke out of one side of my mouth, with a cigarette hanging out of the other side. I modelled my gait on Alan Ladd's for one week, and then maybe Humphrey Bogart's for the next, and then, who knows, maybe Gary Cooper's.

I remember heading up towards the then tiny rural village of Stillorgan, with a cigarette in my mouth, to meet my friends in the Ormonde Cinema. Now you may remember that film stars used to light a cigarette, then get some idea and squint up their eyes as they withdrew it from their lips, dropping it to the ground and stamping it out before they moved off.

Just as I reached the main road, I squinted, withdrew the cigarette, dropping it on the ground, making a stamping motion, but also making sure to avoid the cigarette. I then picked it up and scuttled across the road. I had only the one cigarette. By God, but those Americans were impossibly rich!

My classmates were besotted with the girls who attended Sion Hill Convent, beside our school, and I just couldn't share their fantasies. It wasn't that I didn't like my classmates. They were cleverer than I was, and really nice lads. It was just that I was a year older at a point where a year seems like an aeon.

At this stage I had an idea which gave me a ray of hope. There was a 'grinder's' college on Cross Avenue, just behind Sion Hill, where the girls smelt of perfume and wore lipstick. My God, the wild eroticism of it! A 'grinder's' was an independent college where you could study for examinations outside the usual college system. If I could sit the matriculation examination in the summer of fifth year at Blackrock College, and pass it, I would be free to go to university.

My parents were quite receptive to the idea of my sitting the matriculation. After all, Frank was showing some initiative at last. Sure God was good, and who knows, some good might come of it. I heard my mother saying on the phone: 'Sure it'll keep him off the streets for the summer, and sure maybe he might get a couple of subjects out of it.'

I retired to my room saying to myself: 'Oh no Mother, this is my idea, all my own idea. I'm going to get this exam for my own purposes, and not to prove anything to you.' I was angry that I had had to take my fate into my own hands, without an adult's help.

I went to the grinder's and discovered one very simple thing: my memory was as good as anybody else's. I had never realised that memory was such a great tool. At school, I was so far behind that it seemed futile to try and learn little bits of subjects by heart.

There was little chance for me at my stage to try and understand everything, so I learned off great tranches of poetry, both English and French, and an amazing amount of Virgil's *Aeneid*. The odd thing was that, once learned by heart, they somehow became intelligible. Linguistic resonances began to fall into place, and some primal instinct took over. I actually began to understand what I was learning!

I had been pretty rotten at Latin in school, but I fell in love with it through Virgil, and actually took it as one of my subjects in college afterwards.

The outcome was that I passed the matriculation in five subjects, and became one of only two boys in the college qualified to go to university.

In Blackrock College, conformity was considered a kind of moral virtue in itself. If you made the right noises and were just like the other boys, life was comfortable. It is quite easy to bully clones. So deep was this tradition, that believe it or not, two of the priests from the College visited my father during my matriculation summer, and tried to prevail on my parents to dissuade me from sitting the examination, because it would 'upset the other boys'. Try that for conformity!

I was forced to spend sixth year at senior school after this, but after that I never set foot in the school again, except to support my boys at school events, and attend parent–teacher meetings. When the boys were at the school, I tried not to load them with my baggage, and they both enjoyed their time there and were highly successful on many fronts.

On the conformity issue there was one eminent and enlightened priest, who taught us in sixth year. He used to warn against the phenomenon of 'jeering', explaining that it arose from an unreasoning instinct. He told us of how one boy had become such a victim of this, that when he turned out to play in the senior handball final, a huge number of boys turned out to jeer him.

This wonderful priest was so enraged by this victimisation that he stopped the handball game, and put the mob to shame with a severe reprimanding. The postponement of the final put an end to the jeering and shamed the mob. This man had a heroic sense of faith.

9

Rebirth

I was not disappointed in my expectations of university. I thought I had died and gone to heaven. University College Dublin was situated in what is now the National Concert Hall, in Earlsfort Terrace, and part of what is now known as Charlie Haughey's 'Chas Mahal', the College of Science in Merrion Street. There was something wonderful in having Stephen's Green to stroll in, the Green Cinema for stolen film watching time, Grafton and Dawson Street for coffee shops, as well as Leeson Street for pubs.

'Freshers' Day' was most exciting with all the various societies setting out their stalls. I wandered around and was attracted to the Boxing Club stall. I signed the necessary papers and then asked the big chap who was in charge, who I might be fighting. 'Well,' he said, 'at your weight, you're just inside my class, so you would be fighting me.' The big chap was Hugh Byrne, who would later become a TD. I tore up the papers and departed, wandering over to the Dramsoc (Dramatic Society) stall. I don't know what attracted me to it, but it changed my life irrevocably. Here was something quite unlike school drama, pithy stuff: Yeats, Synge, Tennessee Williams, Christopher Fry, and God knows what else. Unlike school drama, this was my property, and I revelled in it.

I had decided to study law, and to take my Bar exams as well, as I knew that I had an aptitude for the subjects involved. I loved philosophy, history and Latin, and subjects like politics. I had little or no ability for mathematical subjects.

At my first history lecture I was shocked and thrilled to hear Professor Dudley Edwards proclaim that, according to Lecky (the historian), you only had to throw a stick over a workhouse wall to hit one of Daniel O'Connell's bastards. 'Hah,' I thought, 'this is how history should be taught!' Hitherto, history had been merely a series of dates and battles.

I took care to attend the library every day to study for an hour or so, right from the very beginning. I had learned to study only recently, and I knew that I would have to perfect the technique. Actually the history library was a great place to 'hang out'. When you came out for a cigarette break, you met the likes of Maeve Binchy, or Owen Dudley Edwards (son of the late professor) and many others, for mischievous jokes and gossip.

In college I was free to fly. I wasn't just 'one of the Kelly boys' (my two brothers had preceded me through the school). New friendships were struck up. There was rugby, where I could make a fresh start, and holiday work, at a series of jobs in England. These friendships, and the constant exchange of views and debate of issues with new people were as formative as many of the subjects I studied. Also there was hitch-hiking around Europe, which might be considered too dangerous today.

Dramsoc brought me a charmed life. Most people had to establish their identities in this new world, but in Dramsoc there was that fortunate coincidence of the right people coming together at the right time. Two of our political satirical revues were highly successful, so much so that heavy political guns from the Dáil benches appeared in the front row on several nights. Now that was real recognition! They were mainly written by Fergus Linehan, who was a huge driving force, and far ahead of his years in his devastating satirical observations.

He is still writing brilliant satire, and has written a couple of successful books, particularly 'Under The Durian Tree', a most evocative picture of the demise of the Empire way of life in what is now Malaysia.

So it happened that, in a college of some ten thousand students, nearly everybody knew the cast members. This made social life very pleasant indeed. It was customary for the various staff faculties to ask members of Dramsoc to entertain at staff dinners. Thus, you were soon on first name terms with many of the lecturers, and on fairly close terms with many of the professors as well. I was frequently poured out of a lecturer's car outside the gates of my home.

One wasn't paid in cash for these entertainments, but in free drink. At one such dinner I decided to explore the joys of cognac.

I drank it, almost draft, for the entire evening, and was poured out once again at the gate. Unfortunately the evening had ended earlier than the accustomed time, and my family were gathered together in the kitchen, having various pre-bed snacks and hot drinks, as was their custom. I appeared in the kitchen doorway, beaming broadly.

'Well,' said my mother, 'how did the evening go?'

I bowed graciously, but discovered that I had completely lost the power of speech. It wasn't that I would slur if I spoke. No, it was just that my brain wouldn't let me speak. My mother, God bless her, just advised me quietly to go to bed at once. I was only in the bed, when there she was with a glass of hot milk, and powerful painkillers. The subject was never mentioned again. She was a very broad-minded woman for a non-drinker.

I was studying for a B.C.L. degree, but a friend of mine tipped me off that it was possible to combine the lectures for the degree with the Bar lectures. There was a bureaucratic chink which was later closed, but it enabled me, and I think two others, to complete the degree and the Bar in under four years. The degree final was in the spring and the bar final was in the autumn.

Thus, it was necessary to scuttle from afternoon lectures, at 3 p.m., right across the Liffey by a labyrinth of streets to the north city, and the King's Inns. It took some doing, but it was worth it. I would catch up that year which had been stolen from me long ago.

I decided to become an actor two years before the end of my law studies, but I was determined to complete them. I have a thing about that. Once I have begun something I like to complete it. This is not to say that I haven't had loads of failures in my life, but I will stagger on as long as I can, bloodied but unbowed.

One of our revues, *Easy Terms*, was so successful, that it was decided to mount a professional production in the Eblana Theatre, which occupied the basement of the Busáras, Dublin's main bus station. This re-emerged under the title *Fair Game*.

It was a great success, and gained the cast 'provisional' membership of Equity, the Irish union representing actors, directors, and stage and set designers. You had to be a union member in those days to perform in a professional theatre company, and you could apply for membership if you convinced them that you intended making the theatre your career, and then you had to log up so many speaking parts, and so many lines.

This was followed later by a musical, called *Glory Be!*, written by Fergus Linehan, which was really the first broad satire about the emergence of the new state. There were lyrics like:

> What did you do in the Troubles Daddy?
> What did you do back in 1916?
> Were you fighting like a tiger or were you a lamb?
> Well there's really no one now who gives a damn!

This was considered highly irreverent stuff at the time, really daring! No one had ever poked fun at our 'Troubles' heroes, with the exception of *Dublin Opinion*. The country needed to be able to laugh at some sacred cows, and audiences just flocked to the Olympia Theatre nightly.

At this time, what with the theatre at night and lectures in both UCD and the King's Inns, there was little time for actual study. One afternoon during the run of the show, I had to run through the biting wind from UCD to the Inns, and made it just in time for the property lecture by the formidable but loveable Professor Fanny Moran, who was also Regis professor of Law at Trinity College. There was a huge coal fire in the lecture room, and what with overwork and coming in out of the freezing cold to the warmth, I promptly fell asleep, snoring loudly.

Fanny Moran forbade my colleagues to wake me. 'Just leave him,' she said, and one or two precious members of my class waited in delicious anticipation of my execution when I would wake up. These 'precious' ones were already practising the affectations which they hoped to take with them to the Bar. I quite despised them. They tended to stand on their tippy-toes and wring their hands when excited.

When I finally came to, Fanny descended on me with, 'Well Mr Kelly, would you kindly explain the "Rule in Shelly's Case" to us?' I improvised gamely for quite some time, talking absolute bullshit, before she interrupted me with, 'Mr Kelly, I can tell you that I enjoyed your performance last night a hell of a lot more than I did today!' I could see the disappointment on the faces of those who had hoped that I would be thrown out of the class.

She was a fascinating old lady, who had been an observer at the Nuremberg Trials, and who had studied in America during Prohibition. She used to delight her classes every year with accounts of how you could tell when the young American men had been drinking forbidden spirits. 'When you would dance with them', she would say, 'you became aware of this huge lump in the front of their trousers. They had the stuff hidden, you see,' and she would be quite unaware that the entire class was ready to explode with suppressed giggles.

Mind you, that was her only show of naivety. From time to time, there were the remains of what must have been quite a flirt in her, and I think that she was quite mischievous.

I lived in a petrol green sweater for most of my student days. It had seen a lot of wear and there was a barely discernible hole in one elbow. I could never see the point of wearing out good clothes on lecture room desks. I was very fond of it anyway, but one day I was taken aside by one of the 'precious brethren', who told me that he had been deputed to tell me that my 'sartorial standards' were not quite up to those of the King's Inns. My two-word reply made it quite clear that I didn't care what they thought.

Sometimes I think that Fanny Moran divined their attitude to my clothing and coarse way of life in the theatre, because she twisted their noses beautifully one day. My father had been in hospital for tests, and I gained possession of the family car while he was there. It was quite prestigious at the time, being an upmarket Vauxhall Wyvern. I used to drive it up Henrietta Street, turn, and park it with two wheels up on the high kerb outside the students' entrance.

One day, after our lecture she said to me in a loud voice: 'Mr Kelly, are you still driving that handsome Vauxhall car I saw you arriving in the other day?'

'Yes Professor,' I replied.

'Well then, may I beg the favour of a lift down to Trinity College?'

'I would be delighted Professor.'

'Very well then, would you please carry my books for me?'

And I carried her books and my briefcase as she accompanied me out to the car. As we drove off, I wondered why she was smiling to herself, and then I looked in the rear-view mirror to see a couple of the 'precious ones' peeping around the granite pillars behind us.

It was time for me to settle down for my final run towards the Bar finals, as I had just ten weeks left. I was replaced in *Glory Be!* by Terry Brady, who went on to join the cast of *Beyond The Fringe*, and to write shows for the BBC.

10

Love and Love's Haunts

On completion of my Bar exams I went straight into the theatre. My father and my mother had been keen theatregoers, and my mother had a particular passion for it, so much so that when she was a young girl, she and a friend of hers used to picnic in St Stephen's Green Park just to see Hilton Edwards and Micheál MacLiammóir promenade through at lunchtime, apparently unaware of the attention they were attracting, although from my later experience of them, they would have been quite aware.

One of my first theatrical engagements was in Bertholt Brecht's *Saint Joan of the Stockyards*, starring Siobhán McKenna and an American actor named George Mathews. Siobhán was her usual excellent self, but Mathews was a riveting actor. If you look at old black and white Paramount movies, you will see him with great regularity in the background as a tough cop, with a pugilists's face and deep dimple in his chin.

He was of the American school of acting, which works so well in the movies. He never appeared to be acting, and had that stillness which works so well on camera. I had to rush onstage to him as a young detective, with an update of the riots in the cattle yards, and he would say: 'Where the hell have you been?'

He looked so fierce and intimidating that I could hardly get my first line out. I felt like apologising for being late. He was so completely 'real'.

It was during this production that I met my wife, Bairbre. I spotted her immediately at rehearsals. She had huge, brown, Spanish-looking eyes, and glossy dark brown shoulder-length hair. Somebody told me that she was a widow, but I was quite undeterred by this. If anything it heightened her allure. I learned that she had two lovely little girls, aged three and four. I had come from a family which was besotted with babies. We all loved and celebrated them, and do to this day.

I am proud to say that we inherited this from my father and mother. Although my father wasn't very reachable emotionally at a later stage, by me at least, he loved small children. My parents were wary of my new romantic involvement, but when they met the two little girls they just melted into acquiescence.

During the run of the production, our romance blossomed. There is a double set of doors between the green room area and the stage in the Gaiety Theatre, the idea being to prevent backstage noise from reaching the wings. Bairbre and I found ourselves confined in this space, and fell into each other's arms, kissing passionately. We were interrupted by the late Christopher Casson, who apologised profusely, giving us time to vacate the confined space with some grace.

Christopher was a truly delightful man, with a fund of terrifically funny stories about his early years in the theatre. He was the son of the great Shakespearean actors, Sir Lewis Casson and Dame Sybil Thorndike. He told me that when he was a child, playing in the gardens of the ancestral pile, in the English countryside, a gardener who worked for his parents said to him: 'Some day Oi'm goin' up to London to see your parents, jumpin' through their flamin' 'oops!'

It took Bairbre and me three years before we could afford to marry, but we managed it, and now have seven grown children and seventeen grandchildren.

A couple of haunts stand out clearly in my memory from our courtship days. The Trocadero restaurant, on Trinity Street, was one. It was an affordable and welcoming place for cash-strapped actors, and was then owned by a huge Greek man, named Eddie Stephanides, who would join you at your table for a chat, and was reputed to be a huge gambler. Legend had it that he was part of a prestigious poker school, which even included the Taoiseach, Seán Lemass, at one stage.

Another eatery was The Golden Orient restaurant, on Leeson Street, run by Mike Butt, who was subsequently to become Indian Consul. This was where impoverished actors could get one portion of vegetable curry between two people, and Mary Cassidy, the much-loved maître d', was very generous with the side salads.

One evening when Bairbre and I went there it was raided by the Gardaí, in search of wine being drunk after midnight, which was illegal at the time. The advent of the Gardaí had been anticipated, and all the wine had been whipped away to the kitchens. I have rarely seen a funnier sight than huge Gardaí crawling under the tables in search of hidden wine. They gave up in despair amidst the laughter of the patrons.

Famous people I remember seeing there include Nina and Frederik ('Listen to the Ocean'), and Tommy Cooper, one of the funniest men who ever lived. They were appearing in the Theatre Royal, in Hawkins Street.

Then there was Gaj's restaurant (pronounced 'Guy's'), on the top floor of a building on Lower Baggot Street, where you could get delicious stuffed pork steak for a pittance. It would be easy today to say that things were just cheaper back then, but they were never as cheap as they were in Mrs Gaj's. I don't know how she did it. There is no comparable value around at present, even allowing for the enormous inflation since.

It seems a pity that all good restaurants in Ireland just fade away. They have a life with one proprietor, and then they wilt and die. It is still possible to go into a restaurant in the Rhone Valley and be served by the third generation. The simple explanation is that Irish restaurants fade away because their margins on food are just too tight, but is that not just too simple? Does this mean that French restaurateurs lead lives of abject poverty? I think not. One thing is sure: if Ireland had a reputation for being a cheap place to eat, our tourist figures would probably double.

Groome's Hotel, opposite the Gate Theatre, was a great late night drinking spot. It was a wonderful place to gather after a show. Joe Groome was Fianna Fáil treasurer, and his wife, Pattie, was a wonderful hostess, keeping order with a skilful hand and when required, an iron fist.

It was patronised by actors of international fame, politicians of all major parties, and even government ministers (including one Minister for Justice), as well as members of the judiciary and senior counsel.

It was the scene of nights of great fun. I well remember when the Inter-Parliamentary Union was bringing politicians from Northern Ireland to Dublin, before the Troubles had really got going, Bairbre and I joining in a great circle in the small hours, which included John Taylor, John Hume, Gerry Fitt and several Irish TDs, to sing 'The Sash', 'The Ould Orange Flute', as well as 'Danny Boy' and 'Down By The Glenside'. Things have changed since! I wonder would Lord Kilclooney have remembered that persona.

I was appearing in a play in the Gate Theatre, when Bairbre, heavily pregnant with our latest prodigy, arrived to collect me at the theatre. She had been delayed getting into town in her ancient Volkswagen Beetle, and I had gone across the road to Groome's, where I knew she would find me. There were hooligans in the street harassing her in the car, banging on the roof and wings; truly brave carry-on by our gallant fellow misunderstood countrymen. A young Garda saw her predicament and went to her aid. They fled and she got out of the car.

As he escorted her down the street, she was becoming more and more embarrassed, because she was headed for the hotel, where we were going to drink after hours. There was a secret knock for initiates, with a coin on the glass of the front door. As they drew level with it, the Garda looked sideways at her and asked quietly: 'Do you know the knock?'

There were other great musical nights as well. Luke Kelly would occasionally produce the banjo and rouse us all with, 'Take Me Up To Monto' and 'The Ould Triangle'. Sometimes, when there was a really good spontaneous atmosphere, Pattie Groome would appear with bowls of coddle on the house. She liked nothing more than genuine good fun.

There were young lads who worked as waiters in the place, who looked far too young for the late hours. One of these was seen at the Curragh Races one afternoon in a smart crombie coat, looking very prosperous indeed. It was getting late, and this Groome's hotel patron was wondering how the lad would get back in time for his work in the hotel. It was a long way from base, with no transport available to him. The good man offered him a lift back to Dublin, but the lad declined, saying that he would take his chances on making it back in time.

Later that evening, the man was in Groome's, when he saw the lad looking very chipper and on top of his game. He approached two Americans, who had ordered an Irish whiskey and a Scotch whiskey with a dash of soda in it, through the packed and noisy lounge. As he came near them, he lowered his ear to a tray, and then lifted his head again, presenting them with their drinks. One American asked him how he was able to decide which one was neat, and which had the soda in it. 'Ah,' says the lad, 'when I put me head down, I can hear the bagpipes!' The Americans were bemused.

The punter from the Curragh was witness to this and he called the lad over, asking him how he had been able to tell the difference between the drinks. 'Ah,' says the lad, 'sure when I put me head down, sir, I could hear the soda fizzin'.'

'And how did you get back from the Curragh?' asked the punter.

'I got meself a taxi just after I left ye, sir,' says the lad.

As he departed, the punter looked after him ruefully, saying: 'Three days up from the Aran Islands, and he has us all by the bollix!'

There were dramatic nights, too, like the one when Seán Burke, who claimed to have liberated Kim Philby, the spy, from prison, actually fired a revolver through the ceiling to emphasise a point.

One night, when there was a Justice Minister in the interior room, and the evening was just revving up, the place was invaded by an over-zealous young Garda, who began to take the names of the after-hours drinkers. He began in the usual way: 'Name?' 'Joe Bloggs.' 'Profession?' 'Actor,' etc. Having made his way through a succession of people and warned them that they were all likely to be prosecuted for being 'found on' after hours, he reached one small, seated figure.

'Name?' 'Donagh MacDonagh.' 'Profession?' 'District Justice.'

Visibly shaken, the young guard pocketed his notebook, saying: 'If yez are not all out of here in twenty minutes, there's goin' to be real trouble!' He scuttled out the door and wasn't seen again.

There is no justifying the illegality of drinking after hours in a licensed premises, but Lord it was fun! It showed the need for some place for people who work late to foregather. Yes, there are clubs to provide for certain kinds of late night drinking, but somehow nothing has ever taken the place of Groome's.

Maybe part of its charm was that it was strictly illegal, and Irish people of all walks of life get a little thrill of being just outside the law. Also one had the feeling of 'belonging', once accepted. If you ever broke Pattie's rules, that was it for you. There was no getting back in.

Pattie used to do a certain amount of moral policing. When I would appear a few times on my own, she would ask me how Bairbre was getting along, and then suggest to me that it was getting late, and that maybe I should be on my way. When I would reappear with Bairbre, her greeting would signal her approval.

When Christmas time came, Joe Groome would go around and serve everybody personally with champagne as a mark of his appreciation of their custom. We shall not see its like again.

11

Ink

When I began my theatrical acting career, I had acquired an agent, who was fashionable at the time, but who was really a snobbish little rich boy. I got off to a good start, being offered work in my own right, but having an agent seemed to have a 'professional' ring about it.

I waited for the phone to ring, but it just didn't. Hitherto, I had thought that a genius like me could never be out of work. This state of things continued for some weeks until, one Saturday morning, I encountered the late Jack Jones, a journalist with a heart of gold, formerly of the *Irish Press*, and later of the *Irish Times*. He asked me what I was doing and I told him that I was out of work. He took me to the Scotch House on Burgh Quay (now gone), where we met the assistant editor of the *Irish Press*, Fintan Faulkner, over a drink.

It was customary for struggling barristers at the time to do casual work on newspapers, to help make ends meet, and Fintan, hearing that I had qualified for the Bar, offered me work, starting on the following Monday evening. I was able to satisfy my conscience as a freelance actor because I could tell myself that the work was only temporary. The weeks went by, and there was still no offer of theatre work.

One day, while heading down the quays to the *Irish Press*, I met my 'agent', who asked me what I was doing. I told him that, because he had been unable to find me work, I was working as a temporary sub-editor on the newspaper.

'Hmmmmmmmph,' he mused, 'that's rather strange. I never think of actors as being particularly employable people.' That ended our relationship.

Sub-editing was quite highly paid by the standards of those days. I was earning eighteen guineas a week, very nice thank you! The snag was that once you became skilled at it, they offered you a staff job at a pittance. There was still no theatre work, and I just had to survive.

Thus, I became a ten pounds a week hack. I enjoyed the company of my companions on the news desk, but the management were horrible, running the place in a reign of terror. The reign was offensive to me, because I had travelled a bit, and worked at a few strange things. I was a spoilt university pup, and was not going to be intimidated.

One evening I arrived at the desk to be told: 'The assistant editor is gunning for you.' I asked the nature of my crime, but was told smugly by the messenger that he didn't know, but that 'I would soon find out.'

'Then', I said, 'I had better go and find him and ask him what I have done wrong.' 'Oh no, I wouldn't do that,' I was told. This was too much, and I set off in search of the assistant editor, one Michael Mahon, a charming Sligo man (there were two assistant editors). My knock on his door was met with a booming 'come in', and I entered to discover the nature of my crime.

'I believe you wanted to see me, Mr Mahon.'

He brandished a copy of the previous day's newspaper, pointing to a picture caption, and asking, 'What is the meaning of this?'

I looked at the offending caption, and immediately saw that there was an error in it.

'Is this your fine work?' he asked.

'Yes,' I replied.

'And can you explain it.'

I decided to risk all.

'Yes sir, I made a complete bollix of it.'

He looked at me with suspicion for a moment, and then burst out laughing.

'My God,' he said, 'my job would be so much easier if people would only admit their mistakes!'

He always treated me with great charm and courtesy after that.

The biggest drawback, working on a daily paper, was having to work on Sunday evenings. It was completely out of rhythm with my previous social life. The youngsters in the 'Press' never got Sundays off when their leave came up. You got a few days off together, but there was never a Sunday included, unless you were a greybeard.

I was finishing a butt in the doorway of the *Irish Press* offices on Burgh Quay one Sunday evening, before going in to work. There was a man in a battered old hat and raincoat in the doorway beside me. He looked as though he was sheltering from the rain.

The offices always attracted a motley crowd, because there was a readily available gents' toilet once you got past the front counter, nobody could ask you your business, because crowds of employees were always passing through.

There was a mutter from under the battered hat of: 'Bad evening isn't it?'

I replied: 'It would be a whole lot better if I didn't have to go into this hellhole!'

On close inspection, I discovered that my companion was none other than Major Vivion de Valera, managing editor of the Press Group of newspapers. I turned on my heel, and fled indoors. Thanks be to God I never met him again!

Major de Valera was in the habit of accosting employees on the stairs for a spot account of how things were going. One evening he stopped a busy photographer who was going out in a hurry on a news shoot, and asked him: 'What are you on now?'

The answer came back like a shot: 'Twelve pounds a week, sir,' as he sped down the stairs.

I found the reign of terror so humiliating that I decided to look for another job, so I applied to the *Irish Independent*. So bad was the regime in the *Irish Press* that a man was fired for a mistake for which he was not even responsible. The buck should have stopped higher up, but then why should it, when you can find a defenceless underling to fire? So flagrant was the injustice that Douglas Gageby, editor of the *Irish Times*, immediately offered the man a job when he heard the facts, and the job was gratefully accepted.

No job had been advertised in the *Irish Independent*. I had just applied out of the blue, but was granted an interview. When I presented myself, I was offered a job by the editor, no less!

He asked me why I wanted a job with the *Irish Independent*. I told him that I didn't like the regime in the *Irish Press*, that I would prefer to work where you weren't expected to be afraid all the time.

'Right, when you have served your notice with the *Irish Press*, you can start with us,' was the reply. So great was the rivalry between the Independent and the Press groups that I felt that he was secretly pleased at the prospect of a young cub defecting to his newspaper.

When I gave in my notice to the *Irish Press* I was summoned to the editor's office, where he threatened to 'black' me with every other publication in Ireland. He said that I was a 'trainee', and that I hadn't finished my apprenticeship. I am now much older than he was at the time, and I can't see myself making threats against a mere kid.

Change can be effected in mysterious ways. Shortly before I left the *Irish Press*, we were all finding the toilet facilities appalling. As I have said, they were readily available to the general drinking public of Burgh Quay. They were in a horribly unhygienic state, and stayed that way, in spite of complaints from the staff.

One of my colleagues was one Brian O'Neill, who was a staunch trade union activist, and seemed to have settled for that role, at the cost of promotion. He was a crack sub-editor, with a huge store of general knowledge, and handled many of the most volatile and difficult stories.

One evening, there was a bishop in full canonicals, brought down for interview from the State Apartments in Dublin Castle. He was wearing the full purple gear, slippers and all. The Editor asked Brian to show the bishop to the toilet, meaning the Editor's toilet, of course. But Brian, being true to the cause, shepherded the holy man down to our horrific toilets. There were builders reconstructing them the following Monday.

The *Irish Independent* was sheer joy in comparison to the *Irish Press*. There was a happy atmosphere. The chief sub-editor at the time was Dick Roche, and he always left me with my dignity intact no matter what I had done wrong. He was officer material, with the knack of being one of the blokes.

12

Where were You when You Heard the News?

Being a sub-editor in those days could be pretty humdrum until some dramatic story broke, and then the rule was that you had to stay with it and see it through, even if you were a junior. I only once took the 'early turn'. This was usually the privilege of the elderly staff, nearing retirement, whose shift finished at about 10 p.m., but on this particular night, most of the staff were attending an annual drinking marathon freebie, hosted by CIÉ, for all the press. Most people would arrive for work after this event, with more than a little piss-elegance in their demeanour. I opted to take the early shift, and to give the freebie a miss.

I was all alone in the newsroom when the wire copy started to come in. There were two sources: Associated Press and United Press International (A.P. and U.P.I.). On checking the copy I couldn't believe my eyes. It said 'John F. Kennedy shot dead in Dallas, await confirmation.' I checked the two sources and they both told the same story. Then the information was confirmed. I shook with fear at the knowledge that I was the only person in the building who knew the terrible news.

Trembling, I approached the Editor's office door. I knocked gingerly, and was summoned inside, clutching the precious wire copy.

'Well, Mr Kelly, what do you want?'

'Sir, according to U.P.I. and Associated Press, President Kennedy has been shot dead in Dallas.'

The editor looked at me for some time, breathing heavily, and said: 'You'd better be right about this!'

Something told me that I wouldn't remain in journalism in the long run. When I think about the culture of Irish management, I always remember that moment. I had to stay with the gruelling story until the following morning at 11 a.m., along with Seán Cronin, who took over the labyrinthine home story. Kennedy had visited Ireland not that long before, and there were relatives and close friends springing out of the ditches. Afterwards, the editor congratulated the staff on their sterling performances. Ironic when you think that so many of the staff were pissed that night.

After a year in the Indo, I saw an advertisement for a job as a feature writer in the then R.T.V. Guide, and applied at once. Once again, I got an interview, and accepted the job. I lied during the interview, saying that I could type (a skill which hadn't been required as a sub-editor). I worked out my notice in the Indo and realised to my horror that my job began on the following Monday, and I still couldn't type.

I borrowed a typewriter from my girlfriend Bairbre, and typed all day on Friday, Saturday and Sunday, and I mean all day each day for those three days. Sheer terror is a great motivation, and it is amazing what you can learn in a short time. I can type quite well and quite quickly today, but, to my shame, I have never learned to 'touch type'.

My stay in the R.T.V. Guide was not a happy one. The editor questioned my every utterance until I was like a rabbit caught in headlights. I felt so abused. So bad did our relationship become that he gave me a choice between becoming a sales representative for the magazine or getting the sack. I had got engaged shortly after joining the Guide, and Bairbre and I got married about six months later. Here I was, married, with a wife and two little girls, and faced with destitution. I had no choice but to accept his 'kind' offer.

While I was 'on the road', I teamed up with David Hanly, with whom I had formed a close friendship in the editorial room of the Guide, to write a sponsored radio programme for Glen Abbey Knitwear. We modelled it on the *Jack Jackson Show*, which was hugely popular at the time on Radio Luxembourg, but other commitments overwhelmed David after a while and he dropped out.

In this primary incarnation of the *Glen Abbey Show*, David and I received a tape at Christmas time from a man with the name, coincidentally, of Harry Christmas, who was an executive with E.M.I. in Dublin. The tape featured a new pop group from Liverpool, called The Beatles. It was called 'A Christmas Greeting From The Beatles', but it was full of non-sequiturs and incoherent nonsense. We didn't use it, because it would have been incomprehensible to the audience.

The Beatles hadn't become famous yet, and no one could have guessed their potential at the time. Nowadays that tape would be worth quite a lot of money, but hey, how were we to know?

The impresario, Tom O'Donnell, gave us access to the most amazing selection of celebrities for interview on the programme: singer Matt Monroe, comedian Victor Borge, singer Roy Orbison, and our big coup: none other than the late great Ella Fitzgerald. The interview with Ella went beautifully. She was such a gracious lady. I thanked her for appearing on the show, and she said: 'It has been my pleasure, Glen,' thinking, quite reasonably, that my name was Glen Abbey.

When I interviewed Victor Borge in his suite in the Gresham Hotel, he spoke to me for half an hour with no show of impatience, and showed me out with great courtesy. I got back to base, only to find that the tape recorder had malfunctioned. I was heartbroken. There was nothing for it but to try my luck again. I returned, fully expecting to be brushed off.

The door opened and there was the comic genius himself. I told him what had happened, and he was most sympathetic, ushering me in for another half-hour session. 'Never mind,' he said, 'these things happen to everyone. Now let's check the tape, just to make sure, shall we?' Everything was OK, and he sent me on my way, wishing me much success in my career.

Roy Orbison proved to be an interesting character. He told me stories about his constant touring throughout the US. I was intrigued by the rumours of his being an albino: that the hair and the eyebrows were dyed, and that he wore dark glasses to conceal the colour of his eyes. If these things were true, it was one hell of a good disguise.

Once, when he was driving his car along one of those featureless and endless roads across the US, a cop pulled him over for speeding. Orbison told me that there was no soft-soaping those cops. They were renowned in that particular area for being unreachable when it came to pleading for mercy. Orbison pulled over to the hard shoulder of the road, produced his driver's licence on request and then sat in absolute silence.

The cop told him his speed, saying: 'We don't take any prisoners here, buddy.' Then he flipped Orbison's licence open. There was a pause, and the cop said: 'Are you *the* Roy Orbison?'

'That depends, officer,' said Roy. 'I am certainly the person on that licence.'

'Hell,' says the officer, 'you are my idol! Mr Orbison I can't give you a ticket. Wait till I tell my buddies that I met *the* Roy Orbison! Mind how you go, sir. This has been great day for me!'

Many years later I met Tom O'Donnell and asked him why he had been so kind to David and myself, giving us access to such an array of international artists. He told me that he was highly amused at our youth and enthusiasm. 'You will never know how young you both looked,' he said, and of course we thought that we had looked like grown-up men out in the big, bad world. There certainly wasn't much incentive for him to give us access to all his artists, because our show was only at the embryonic stage.

After David dropped out, I decided to go it on my own. It was extremely difficult to get recording time to fit my travelling schedule, and even more difficult to write the show while on the road, but it was recorded somehow every week for three years. It was to be reborn in another form a few years later.

One evening as I walked the promenade at Salthill, Co. Galway, I was feeling particularly lonely and desperate, when two little boys passed me on their bicycles. One of them shouted: 'Let's go,' and the other one replied: 'With The Glen Abbey Show!' (our opening catchphrase from the show), and they will never know what they did for my morale!

I was a year on the road when I decided that there was only one cure for my career problem, and that was to resign from the Guide, and go completely freelance as an actor, although by now I had three little girls. When I told Bairbre that I had decided to resign, to her eternal credit, she backed me up to the hilt in this precarious exercise. Her exact words were: 'I never thought that you would have the guts.' I am eternally grateful to her for this. After I resigned, I found that my editor had arranged that I should not be made permanent. Thus, I had no entitlements when I left. No comment.

13

Days of Wine and Roses

Bairbre and I always made a point of having a family holiday, even when we had generated a family of seven children. I discovered Castletownbere, in West Cork, while travelling for the Guide. I had set off in snowy conditions, with ominous warnings of further snowstorms. It is a very long drive to West Cork, and Bairbre was anxious because I was travelling in such bad weather, so she kept phoning the newsroom in RTÉ for updates.

It just about never snows in Castletownbere; something I wasn't yet aware of. It is so far south, and warmed by the Gulf Stream, that the climate is sub-tropical. The saying goes that it never snows beyond Hungry Hill. There are plants which grow in Glengarriff and Parknasilla, which grow nowhere else in the country. Even the seaweed is a bright yellow colour.

I booked into the local hotel in Castletownbere, and after my evening meal, I strolled down the town in balmy conditions to a pub for a few pints. There were Breton fishermen in the pub, and it was their custom to buy whiskey by the bottle, and mark off each man's share on it. These shots were swallowed neat, and another one would be ordered as soon as the previous one was finished, I watched, mesmerised, for the evening.

This was followed by folk dancing on the street outside the pub. I called Bairbre from the phone box and described the incredible scene which I was witnessing. I also told her that I was in my shirtsleeves. She couldn't believe what she was hearing. There had been scenes of huge snowstorms throughout the country on TV, and she was sure that I would be stuck in a snowdrift somewhere.

We decided there and then that this was the place for us. I was to try and book somewhere in the town for our holidays. I asked Imelda Hegarty, who, with her husband Justin, owned the Berehaven Hotel (now gone alas), if she could put us up at a rate which we could afford, and she said that she would be delighted. Believe me, the rate was fabulously cheap. I just couldn't believe my luck.

Thus began a friendship with the Hegartys and many wonderful holidays. Castletownbere was a sleepy place then. It hadn't yet been developed as a deep sea port. There was one jetty pointing out towards Bere Island, and the sea came right up to the back of the hotel garden.

I had the use of a boat for a small fee from a local man, and went out fishing in the bay. The fishing was terrific, and I would return with mackerel and huge skate. I had a friend who worked for Irish Lights, as lighthouse keeper on Bere Island, before the lighthouse was automated. His name was Danny Neill, and he was generous with his time and his boat. He would take me out with him while he baited his lobster pots.

One day we were at the mouth of Bantry Bay, at the Piper Rocks, and I was fishing with a handline when I got a tremendous bite. I was very excited, and let the line run out for a bit, hoping the prey would hook itself properly. Suddenly the line started to go out at an alarming rate. Danny reached over and, to my bewilderment, grabbed the frame and what remained of the line, and threw it over the side.

As he pulled on the starting rope of his engine, he said: 'Ye were over the back of sleeping basking shark there. They often lie on the bottom here. If that lad had taken a notion to head out to sea, ye would have been over the side in no time at all.' It was a good lesson, from a man to respect, who had fished the Newfoundland Banks. I was suitably chastened.

Our evenings were spent in the hotel bar, where there was a really good sing-song every night. For a cash-strapped young actor, it was quite something to take your whole family to a hotel in West Cork each year for a couple of weeks.

So good was the sing-song that a bank clerk, who resided in the hotel, succeeded in locking himself into the bank's vault, while trying to remember the words of a song from the previous night. His manager was not amused.

We used to prevail on one of the participants in the sing-song to sing 'My Heart and I', so that we would witness his top set of dentures dropping out as he sang the third last note: 'My heeaa-aaaart and I.'

One year, when we were about to depart for home, Imelda asked us would we consider straying on for another week free of charge, as our departure would break up the nightly party at the bar. I have never accepted an invitation with such alacrity!

We used to drive out the twelve miles to Allihies, a most picturesque village, clinging to the cliff, where there is a huge copper mine, which was in use well into the twentieth century. The beach is a wonderful golden colour, being composed of the tailings from the mine.

Allihies was renowned at the time for Nonie Martin's pub, where there was a piano, and even better sing-songs. There was a party phone to Allihies, which gave the requisite number of 'dings' to let you know that the call was for you, and this was warning that the motorcycle Garda was on his way from Castletownbere. The Garda would arrive at Bella Connell's pub in Eyries, and when he would leave it the phone would 'ding' for us.

At the signal we would all stand outside, admiring the nocturnal view of the bay below, as we watched the light of the Garda's motorcycle coming through the gap in the mountains. There would be the odd pint glass on a windowsill, to tease him, but no one on the premises.

He would drive his motorcycle menacingly up and down the road among the throng, and then roar off into the night defeated.

We would then watch him disappearing through the only other gap in the hills out of the town, his tail light looking like a tiny cigarette end in the dark. He would be only out of sight when the piano would be going again and the sing-song would recommence.

There was one night when he lost his 'cool' completely. He drove his bike right up close to me, saying: 'Ya needn't think that I don't know that you're drinkin' out here after hours. I'll catch ya yet!' I protested my innocence just to annoy him.

One day an American yacht berthed at Castletownbere after a transatlantic crossing. I happened to be on the jetty, and they threw me the line and I tied her up. When they came ashore, they were looking for a hotel to stay in for a few nights, and they urgently wanted a bath and a meal.

I led them up to the hotel, where they were booked in. The skipper was a cardiac surgeon, and his crew were family members.

After dinner they expressed a desire to see 'a real Irish shebeen'. Now, Nonie's wasn't a shebeen. It was a properly licensed premises, but we told them that it was a shebeen, and offered to drive them out to Allihies for the evening. Several cars went in convoy, ours and the Hegartys', and other cars filled with assorted regulars from the hotel bar. In those days it was permissible to drink and drive. We had a wonderful evening, and even induced the Americans to sing us a Harvard College football song.

Nonie, a lady of mature years, had gone upstairs and changed into her best dress for the occasion, and at one time during the evening, she tried to make her way around the end of a couch, where the hapless bank clerk was seated. She caught her dress on the end of the couch, and feeling the tug thought the worst, and began to beat the bank clerk about the head. It took quite some time to reassure her that she had not been improperly assaulted.

I had insisted on leading the cortège from Castletownbere to Allihies, and was even more insistent on doing so at the end of the evening. We sailed off on convoy again along the road, which at some places comes too close to the cliff edge for comfort. At some stage I took a left turning, which, it transpired, took us into a field. I led the convoy right around the perimeter of the field, with great dignity, and then out on to the road again, and back home again to Castletownbere.

The following morning I woke up with a headache and I reached out beside the bed to where my spectacles should have been. I had left them in Nonie's, and had been flying blind the previous night. That American heart specialist will never know how lucky he was to arrive home safely.

At some point during our regular visits, Castletownbere was graced with a new Garda sergeant. He was very zealous in his duties. But the culture in the town was one which needed to be wooed, not confronted and dominated. I have been told by an old hand that you must win the trust and affection of the local people before you can police effectively. Apparently, if you make yourself something 'apart', you will remain apart, and you won't get much cooperation.

There was a Garda already there, who had never aspired to being a sergeant, and had been in Castletownbere for twenty years. One day, the sergeant, who had only been a couple of weeks in the town, was walking down a lane, when he was pelted with large lumps of mud by local children from behind a hedge. His uniform was ruined, and there was no hope of catching the culprits. It would be like coursing hares on foot in the dark. The sergeant was furious. When he reached the station, he said: 'This is disgraceful conduct. The children are completely out of hand in this town.'

The long-serving Garda turned to him and said: ''Tis the strangest thing now, Sergeant. I don't know what to make of it at all. I've been here twenty years now, and they never did the likes of that to me!'

One time when we were on holiday in Castletownbere, I had been working in the Gate Theatre. I had left Dublin with an easy mind, having been asked by manager Brian Tobin to play roles in three plays, end to end, the following season and I was thrilled with the forthcoming continuity of work.

Towards the end of our holiday, we asked Bairbre's mother to check the state of our house, and to go through the mail. This she did, and we got her to read out the potentially important letters to us. One was from Brian Tobin, telling me that the offer of the parts had been a ghastly mistake. I was not being considered for them, and he was very sorry about it. Not as sorry as I was! This was really going to take the shine off the holiday.

Bairbre and I sat on our bed, frantically trying to think up a strategy. After all, this had not been merely an availability check on the part of the theatre. I considered that it had been a contract, albeit a verbal one, but definitely binding. Then we decided on a course of action. Telegrams were in existence in those days, and we drafted one to the Gate Theatre, saying: 'Looking forward to rehearsals. Arriving from holiday Monday. Frank.'

We enjoyed the rest of the holiday as best we could, and returned to Dublin. I knew that the venue for rehearsals was the Tin Church in Ranelagh, a Dublin suburb, and presented myself for rehearsals at 10 a.m. on the Monday morning, where I was welcomed warmly and a script put into my hand. There was no mention of Tobin's letter, and I played the three parts in the season. We will never know who might have replaced me.

I was often given warnings about the inadvisability of going off on these family holidays. Some important career opportunity might crop up, and I might miss the chance of a lifetime. But we felt that it was worth the risk. As a matter of fact, I never missed anything of importance, and on one occasion, when I was riding high, I turned down a TV commercial because I had booked a house in the West of Ireland.

We went off on holiday, fully prepared to take the financial hit, and grimly reminding ourselves of our family priorities. Low and behold, when we returned after the longest holiday we had ever dared to take, the advertising agency which had offered the commercial was on the phone again. The project had been put on hold (not because of my lack of availability, I hasten to add!), and they were now going ahead with it. Thus I had my cake and ate it.

Now and then there is a sense of empowerment in making your own decisions, even at the risk of financial loss.

14

Lebensraum

Castletownbere was followed by Cleggan, in Connemara, where we used to rent a beautiful bungalow, just up the lane from what was then Eileen O'Malley's pub. You could stroll out the front door, up a slight rise, and view the sunset on Inishbofin in the evenings. It was on what was originally the road to Aughrisbeg, which lost almost all of its male population during the Cleggan disaster, when the whole fishing fleet was taken unawares by a freak local storm. There is a new road now, and what was originally the main road is now merely a muddy lane.

The setting of the bungalow is matchless, and here was I once again an actor living on the clippings of tin, on holiday with my young family. It was a great privilege. I used to fish off the pier, and pick out the sandy spots for the plaice, and fish straight down off the pier for rock bream. I had great success, and Bairbre used a recipe given to her by our landlady, the late great Inishbofin-born Mary Coyne, for a delicious fish pie. I have never tasted anything like it since.

One day I had been fishing away happily, when a crowd of German tourists arrived, and became very excited as I landed a few mackerel. They drove off at speed to Clifden, and returned within an hour, equipped with brand new fishing rods and reels. They must have spent a fortune!

I wasn't in a position to object to their intrusion on my space, which was limited enough, but the crunch came when I turned to see a German youth running towards his companions with a fine fish which I had just caught and left on the ledge behind me. I dropped the rod and ran after him, shouting: 'That fish is mine. Give it back to me at once!' He paid no attention to me, and just sprinted up to his companions, who had a bag on the same ledge.

I reached him ready to do battle, but he just grinned at me and took another fish out of the bag.

'Of course it is your fish, but ours is bigger!'

We went to Cleggan for several years, and have great memories of it, including many trips to Omey Island, which can be reached over the sands at low tide. It is a breathtaking place.

One morning I rose early on a bright sunny day, and drove over to Claddaghduff, which is on the landward side of the sandy causeway to Omey. I tackled up my rod, and essayed a few casts as I made my way up along the coast. I eventually reached a lovely flat rock, ideal for casting.

I was completely preoccupied, trying to disentangle a bird's nest of fishing line, when I nearly jumped out of my skin. Something had tapped my shoulder. When I turned, there was the German youth. He bowed and said: 'I think you are standing on my spot. I was here yesterday.' I would love to be able to tell you that I said something crushing and eloquent, but suddenly the humour of the situation struck me, and I burst out laughing. I couldn't even get a word out to argue with him, and he retired, shaking his head and convinced that I was a madman.

When the house became unavailable in Cleggan, we rented what was known as 'The Steps House', in Roundstone, further along the coast, on the other side of Clifden. It still stands out because of the long flight of steps to its front door. It was in the front room bay window of this house that I used to work every morning, polishing the final draft of a comedy novelette, *The Annals of Ballykilferret*. Then off to Gurteen beach for the afternoon, and pints in O'Dowd's pub in the evenings.

As I unloaded the car when we arrived for our holiday, the children, who had been solemnly enjoined to do their own unloading, vanished down the town as soon as the car doors were opened, to renew acquaintances with their friends. One year as I was making yet another trip down the long steps to collect the next pile of children's clothes, I encountered one of my sons, who couldn't have been more than five years of age.

'What are you doing, son?' I enquired.

'I can't stop now,' was the answer. 'We're tappin' a barrel in Vaughan's Pub.' He had got himself a job at sixpence a week from the proprietress of the pub, Carmel Faherty. I'd say he got the sixpences, but I don't think he ever put in the work.

The children never needed to be entertained in Roundstone. There was a ready-made entertainment infrastructure there for them. One year, I sat down to write a newspaper column for the now defunct *Sunday Journal* in the bay window, when I found myself short of a topic. Then I remembered 'The Roundstone Crow', a part albino bird, which was entertaining everyone with his antics.

His movements were quite uncoordinated, and he was shunned by the other birds, who were sat in a row, some distance away from him on the telephone wires.

Every now and then his balance mechanism would go awry, and he would fall backwards, but he would not relinquish his hold on the wire. Thus he was left hanging upside-down for a few seconds before he flapped his wings and regained his upright position. It looked as though he was doing a trapeze act. I began to give weekly accounts of his antics, and he gained quite a following.

Another example of his bizarre behaviour was to strut along the harbour wall, opposite O'Dowd's pub, and then stand staring at you until he suddenly fell off the wall on to the roadway. He would never have survived without his fan club, who fed him daily. They gave the other birds the bum's rush when they tried to steal his grubstake.

Roundstone was certainly a place of strange happenings. One day I was seated in Vaughan's pub, to where I had repaired to sip a glass of beer, while waiting for the children to get their swimming gear, when a man approached me and bowed in an old-world fashion. He was from nearby Carna, and came with an invitation for me to fight a man from there. I had been appearing on *The Irish Superstars* (often referred to as the 'Milk Superstars'), a sports programme which had been on television. It included nine events of one's choice, and I had come second in the show business section. Apparently this man had been teased almost to the point of insanity by his cronies, who had been telling him that I was a stronger man than he was.

I thanked the messenger solemnly for his invitation, but explained that I had my wife and children in tow, and I could hardly see the matter through with them as an audience. He accepted my refusal with understanding and respect, bowed and made his exit. As I sat in beside Bairbre in the car, I could feel a chill up my spine.

15

Greasepaint

My mother didn't want me to be an actor. She used to say to me: 'But you never go to the theatre. How do you expect to become an actor if you never go to the theatre?' This wasn't exactly true. I did go from time to time, but you will appreciate there hadn't been much time during my student period. My father had taken me as a child to the old Abbey Theatre, which burned down, and then to the Abbey at the Queen's. I had seen Noel Coward and Michael Redgrave in the Olympia Theatre, and many, many other great people, particularly in the Ilsley and McCabe era in that theatre.

I used to say to her: 'But I want to do it. I don't just want to watch it.' I can now see the flaw in my youthful logic, but I have compared notes with actors of some renown, who said the same thing at the same age. The difference was that they had institutions like R.A.D.A. (Royal Academy of Dramatic Art) to develop their skills and theatrical literacy, whereas we really didn't have anything of that standard in those days.

My first inkling of a vocation for the theatre was when I was looking at an old volume of *Dublin Opinion* in which there was a cartoon, showing a clown looking down sadly at a collection of vegetables and bric-a-brac which had been thrown at him. It was an old style stage with gas footlights, and it was an extraordinarily evocative drawing by W.H. Conn, whose work was unfailingly beautiful.

The cartoon was entitled 'The Bird', and something in it struck a chord within me. It looked like a kind of Calvary; a triumph of dignity over ridicule. I didn't link it in any way with the school productions.

My father used to reminisce about what was termed 'a smooth night out', by his Uncle Charlie, who would take him to the old style music hall. Uncle Charlie used heavily scented hair oil, smoked cigars, and sounded like a creation of James Joyce. My father said that there was a wonderful atmosphere about the music hall which could never be recaptured, and I used to invent my own music hall in my mind. When I was small, I thought that the theatre was a music hall. I never imagined that there were such things as plays.

In Ireland one just had to train on the job, to get as much work as possible, and hope to learn as one went along. I was lucky. I got a very wide variety of work. Because I could sing and play the fiddle I found myself on the cabaret circuit, which comprised golf club evenings and corporate functions. The customary fee for this when I started was about five pounds, which later rose to about twenty. This was a considerable addition to very low theatre salaries, and a great help to our home economy when the children were small.

While *Saint Joan of the Stockyards* was playing, I went into rehearsal for a late night Theatre Festival revue in the Gate Theatre, called *Slings And Arrows*. This starred Gerry Alexander, who was President of Equity for many years, Des Keogh, myself, Rosaleen Linehan, and the late Finn O'Shannon, and was directed by Lelia Doolan. It transferred to the Eblana after the festival, and was quite a hit.

A mischievous spirit entered the show, and this led to some very dubious, if amusing, incidents. Then again, I have a friend who was a member of the Royal Shakespeare Theatre for many years, and he told me that there was an outbreak of water-throwing in the company, causing actors and actresses to have to dry their dresses and doublet and hose very shortly before going onstage.

An edict had to be issued that any company member, no matter how famous or prominent, would be dismissed forthwith if the water-throwing continued.

In our show, there had been a series of practical jokes on members of the cast, increasing in daring to a crescendo, where Finn O'Shannon was onstage in a sketch where she had to smoke a cigarette with great languor. She lit it and drew on it, and it exploded in her face. Someone (not me!) had spiked it with one of those practical joke bangers.

Afterwards Finn was in a sate of high indignation in the dressing room. She was unburdening herself of her just rage to Rosaleen Linehan. 'Disgraceful! I've never seen such unprofessional conduct in my life!' She reached for her cigarettes, lit another one, and it exploded in her face. The joker had spiked every cigarette in the packet.

I had played the role of Shawn Keogh in *The Heart's a Wonder*, the musical version of *The Playboy of the Western World*, in a UCD Dramsoc production. It had been very successful in a production in the Gaiety Theatre, which had eventually transferred to London. I wasn't in this, because it clashed with exams, so I was delighted when it came around some years later and I was asked to play Shawn again.

The show starred Milo O'Shea as Christy Mahon, the Playboy, Una Collins as Pegeen Mike, Ann O'Dwyer as The Widow Quinn, and Maureen Toal as Sara Tansey, with Charlie Byrne as Old Mahon.

In Denis Carey we had a talented director, if a little tetchy, and one day I was at rehearsals, on the sidelines with Maureen Toal, when I muttered to her: 'I don't know about you, but I could murder a cup of tea.' Although he was in the middle of a difficult scene, Carey lip-read me, and turned on me, saying that I was damned lucky to be in the show, never mind being given tea. As a very junior member of the company I was quite defenceless, and for once I could think of nothing to say.

Toal came to my aid like a tigress. Who did Denis Carey think he was, attacking a young actor who was a friend of hers? The remark hadn't been addressed to him in the first place, and he must have been using some listening device to hear it. It was high time that we had a cup of tea anyway, and he could go on working if he liked. She routed him completely, and I have always been grateful for that stout defence. It is nice to have a friend when you need one.

Una Collins was divine as Pegeen; beautiful, feisty and sexy as blazes. At the close of the play, she would have the audience in tears as she dismissed me with: 'Quit my sight. Oh my grief, I've lost him surely. I've lost the only Playboy of the Western World!' as the tears ran down her face. What the audience didn't know was that she managed to fit in between 'Quit my sight' and 'Oh my grief', through slack lips, like a ventriloquist, 'ye little bastard, or I'll break your arse!'

The role of Susan Brady was played with great gusto by Lelia Doolan, and when the girls in the show all held hands and did their vigorous dance, Lelia was downstage right in the formation. She looked splendid in her red skirt, bare legs and brogues. She kicked her white bare legs with such vigour and commitment that her right boot flew off and down into the orchestra pit, were it collided with the fiddle of veteran player Bay Jellett.

There was a strange squawk and then silence from the fiddle, as the other instrumentalists soldiered on, and a very young Proinnsías Ó Duinn kept them all cool from the podium. Fortunately there was no real damage done to the fiddle, although as a fiddle owner, it beats me how it wasn't in splinters.

The musical and comedic skills I used on the cabaret circuit also gave me the entrée to the world of the variety theatre, and this gave me greater continuity of work than I would have had otherwise. Variety was frowned on by many 'legitimate' actors, who considered it beneath their dignity, and somewhat vulgar. I remember one night in Groome's Hotel, I was talking to an actor who was draped in a doorway, telling me that he was filming down in Ardmore Studios.

'I only do "legitimate" theatre,' he said, 'not the variety stuff you do.' What he didn't know was that I had been dubbing his dialogue all day, as the director had found his voice and accent unacceptable. It struck me as slightly ironic at the time that he couldn't sing a song, be funny, or play a musical instrument.

Another curious fact is that attempts have been made to teach people how to be funny on some drama courses. I feel that you just can't teach people how to be funny. My friend, Eamon Morrissey (he who is the chief exponent of the humour of Myles na Gopaleen in his one man shows) is a prime example of this. He can do excellent 'straight' work, but if he wants to be funny, something magic happens. If he decides to get a laugh by pouring a jug of milk, you had better not move, because no one will be watching you.

My 'Groome's critic' would have approved of my being cast in a 'legitimate' part, as Haines the Englishman, in *Bloomsday*, Alan McClelland's adaptation of Joyce's *Ulysses*, which was produced by Gemini, Phyllis Ryan's company. Ronnie Walsh played the role of Leopold Bloom, to great critical acclaim. Ronnie was a very erratic actor, and a mite undisciplined, if very talented.

I remember one night when he had completely forgotten his lines in the pub scene, with 'The Citizen'. To our great surprise, he threw a great improvised tantrum, ordering us all out of the pub. We had no option but to depart offstage. There was method in his madness. He was now free to do as he pleased, which he did, to great effect. He outdid Joyce with his sheer creativity.

Afterwards, we had a very distinguished visitor backstage. It was Alec Guinness, no less. He was completely taken with Ronnie's performance, saying that it was one of the best things he had ever seen on a stage. By the way, he had insisted on paying for his tickets on the way in. It was a great pleasure to meet one of my heroes. I had worshipped him from the day I was brought to see *Kind Hearts and Coronets*.

As I have said, my career constantly oscillated between variety and straight theatre. I have had the privilege of working at very close quarters with three very famous Irish comics: Jimmy O'Dea, Jack Cruise and Cecil Sheridan. I got to know them very well, and wrote quite a few sketches for Jack Cruise, as well as one big one for all three of them, with the inclusion of Noel Purcell, for a TV show. The problem was that there was no love lost between any of them, just an atmosphere of seething paranoia. To whom do you give the tag line? A tricky business indeed!

Some divine intervention gave me the answer. Write a sketch where they all say the tag line together! Anything else would have led to blood on the walls. I wrote it, and I don't remember how funny it was, but they never spotted the device.

I worked with Jimmy O'Dea in the Gaiety Theatre in a production of *Mother Goose*. He treated me with unfailing courtesy, even inviting Bairbre and me to a party in his apartment. This was recognition indeed for a young spud!

I was taken out of the chorus and elevated to the status of one-line participant in one or two of the sketches with him in the show. One day I was standing with Jimmy just inside the back door of Neary's Pub, behind the Gaiety Theatre. An aggressive drunk approached me, who had some crow to pluck with me about something he had seen me do onstage. Jimmy intervened like a tiny fighting cock.

He put the aggressor to flight with: 'This young man is a friend of mine, and a "pro" to boot. He is having a drink with me, and if you have anything to say to him, you will speak to me first.' Jimmy, although a tiny man, had enormously wide and penetrating eyes. He was well used to fighting his corner on the variety circuit, and a formidable foe.

The coward fled without uttering another syllable. I felt very proud, because, when you are young, you may decide to be aggressive when you are on your own, but you don't know what to do when in the presence of your betters, and you need a closing of ranks when you are under pressure.

Mother Goose incorporated the use of Duffy's Circus. We had some goats, provided by Tommy Duffy and his lovely wife, Gertie, who were corralled at the back of the stage, in a sunken area near the gents' toilet, and we were asked not to feed them sugar lumps (readily available from Neary's Pub). Of course we couldn't resist the urge to curry favour with the goats, and fed them pounds of sugar lumps. What we didn't know when Tommy Duffy asked us not to feed them sugar, was that it makes them defecate prodigiously.

Part of the circus act consisted of a tightrope walk, during which the goats crossed a narrow bridge of metal on supports, stretching from one side of the stage to the other, just below the proscenium arch. It was quite spectacular, because the metal strip looked for all the world like a rope, from the audience's perspective.

There was a great roll of drums as the goats began their breathtaking journey, and just as they were all in mid-trot, there was shower of excrement which rained on the stage like a hailstorm, and rolled down to the footlights. During the scene which followed, the dancers collected a large amount of goat shit on their shoes.

We cried with laughter, but somehow Tommy Duffy couldn't see the funny side at the time. I can't say I blamed him. He was a true professional.

16

A Touch of Art

I found myself back in legitimate theatre again when I secured a part in *The Voice of Shem*, Mary Manning's adaptation of James Joyce's *Finnegans Wake*, in the Eblana. There is one sure way of getting inside the skin of James Joyce's prose, and that is to recite it aloud, and characterise it in performance. Somehow it just comes alive. One doesn't miss the echoes of things contemporary and ancient, and the sheer genius of its enigmatic rhythms, which it takes several readings of the work to find in the normal way.

Amongst the cast were Paddy Bedford, Pat Fay, Martin Dempsey, Finn O'Shannon, Marie Kean and May Cluskey, and it was directed by Louis Lentin. At one level, the dialogue sounded like something from a nineteenth century lunatic asylum, and yet it was permeated with Joyce's sense of humour and weird logic. There is something about *Finnegans Wake*, which makes one suspicious that the author might have been playing his audience like fish, for sheer mischief.

The most memorable part of the play was the conversation between the two washerwomen, looking out over Dublin Bay from some height ('Saints of light! See there … is that the Poolbeg flasher beyond, far far,' etc.). It was played by Marie Kean and May Cluskey, and their rendition of it would have made Joyce cheer.

One could see Joyce's mental picture of the city with which he was obsessed, and the totality of the picture in 'Riverrun past Eve and Adam's from swerve of shore to bend of bay brings us by a commodious vicus of recirculation back to Howth Castle and environs', as it was spoken at the beginning of the play. I agree with those who say that Joyce must have meant *Finnegans Wake* to be read aloud.

I came to the cast as a naive young actor, and in one scene Louis wanted myself and another actor to mime the 'rowing' of Tim Finnegan's coffin to the next life, on a dais, mid-stage, in cold steel lighting. It was a most effective idea. I started to mime rowing in the most realistic way I could, dutifully feathering my oar between plunges. Louis asked me what I was doing. I replied: 'Rowing, Louis. Why?'

'But', said Louis, 'I wanted *stylised* rowing, for heaven's sake!'

I had no idea what he meant. 'Oh,' I said, 'I thought that you wanted "real rowing".' He was so flabbergasted at my lack of artistic sensitivity that all the cast burst out laughing. To his credit, Louis bore with my naiveté.

The show went to Paris, to my utter joy. I was in a ferment of excitement as the departure day approached. Through some administrative cock-up, when some of us presented ourselves at the bank, we received our entire salaries in advance, as well as our subsistence money.

When impresario Brendan Smith discovered this he was apoplectic with rage. He had visions of profligate actors broke and destitute in Paris, whom he would have to bail out. A famous broadcaster, who was an aspiring actor then, and working part time in Brendan's office, told a cast member that Brendan, who liked to keep fresh fruit in his office, actually smashed a large Granny Smith into the wall when the error was discovered.

When we were on the aircraft, poor Brendan pleaded with some of us to allow him to 'mind' our money for us, but we mischievously declined his kind offer. The show was in a little theatre down on the Left Bank, in Rue d'Écosse. It all felt so bohemian at the time, strolling down the Boulevard Saint-Germain.

The audience surprised us by knowing every word of *Finnegans Wake*, and applauding at places where there had been silence in Dublin. When we met them after the show, we were put to shame by their knowledge of Joyce. Most of us had to bluff wildly. The experience really brought home to us the sophistication of the French.

We also had the great pleasure of meeting Sylvia Beach, of Shakespeare & Co., Joyce's publisher. She was a delightful little woman, with glittering, dark brown eyes, and wispy grey hair. She reminded me of some little woodland creature. Her sense of humour was terrific, and she had time for everybody. In the course of her conversation with us, she said: 'Jimmy was such a naughty boy, you know, such a very naughty boy!' One gathered that this was a reference to her many handouts to the great writer.

We met her later on in Dublin, and she was just as outgoing as she had been in Paris. However, although she was a frail little old lady, one could detect a great inner strength within her. Joyce certainly happened on the right person. Who knows what sort of career he might have had if he had never met her.

Poor Brendan Smith was the butt of a rather cruel practical joke one night in a Paris restaurant. We had all been very generous to ourselves, and when it came to settling the bill, Finn O'Shannon and Paddy Bedford pretended that they and I had run out of money; that we had gone completely broke. Brendan took the bait beautifully. He ranted and raved about the improvidence of actors and how they couldn't be trusted with a sou.

He had warned us that this would happen. Why had we not allowed him to manage our money? Now he was faced with giving us handouts; just as he had feared in the first place! Just as he was reaching maximum blood pressure point, Finn told him that we were only joking. He stood stupefied for a second, and then, to his credit, he laughed heartily, and when Brendan laughed it was memorable. His eyes lit up, and his usually solemn face dissolved into creases of mirth, his head went down and his shoulders shook uncontrollably. We paid his bill by way of atonement.

A journalist from the then *Manchester Guardian* was present in the restaurant that night, and wrote an account of the evening which was like something out of *Punch* magazine in 1890. You would have thought from his description that he had been at Donnybrook Fair, drunk a litre of poteen and encountered a few leprechauns along the way. There had been nothing 'Oirish' whatsoever about the evening. What is it with certain British journalists? They invent their own Ireland, no matter what. The poet John Montague was present that night, and I don't think he would have hung around for a night of Irish Blarney. We found him charming and dignified.

We arrived in Paris, right at the height of the Algerian crisis, when de Gaulle was hanging the *Pieds-Noirs* (the people of French and other European ancestry who lived in French North Africa, namely French Algeria) out to dry. All along the Champs-Élysées there were little concrete pillboxes with gun barrels peeping out, and, here and there, graffiti, which read 'Algérie Française'. Heady Stuff!

One night Paddy Bedford and I were pretty drunk, and wandering up towards the Place du Tertre. We were doing 'Singin' in the Rain' dance routines across the street, when we discovered that the soles of our shoes were covered with sticky fresh tar. Then, to our horror, we discovered that we were dancing on a freshly-painted 'Algérie Française'. Our flight down a side street was mercurial. If the gendarmes had found two foreigners with fresh tar on their shoes at that site, who knows for how long we might have disappeared?

Another night Paddy and I were in the Algerian Quarter (we seemed to have a penchant for danger) when I saw something about which I had only read in Western stories. The door of a café opened and an Algerian man was thrown out, but thrown out horizontally, and I mean horizontally. His senseless body hung for a nanosecond in mid-air, and then dropped to the pavement with a sickening thud. We both fled again.

I felt really cosmopolitan, seated one night in the Café Flore, on the Champs-Élysées, in the very chair used by Oscar Wilde, with 'Rendezvous Des Intellectuelles' written on the wall beside me, my coat draped around my shoulders and a Gauloise smouldering in my hand. I thought: 'What is all this about having to struggle to get to the top? I have reached the top!' I was to land on my rather unprepossessing backside many times after that!

17

Back to Basics

An invitation by Cecil Sheridan, comedian and parodist supreme, to take part in his recreation of the old time music hall in the Eblana Theatre was very welcome. The show, *The Good Old Days*, consisted of the rebirth of all the great names of the old time music hall, and just caught a mood with the public. It was a huge success, running for four months, which was a major run for the Eblana. A baby daughter, my lovely Ruth, was born to us during this show. We were living on the clippings of tin, but we were very happy. An aunt of Bairbre's called to our house in Monkstown to see the new baby and, unfailingly generous as she was, practised the custom of 'hanselling' the baby, by slipping some money under the pillow in the cot.

Bairbre kept her poor aunt talking, while I slipped the money from under the pillow, slid out the back door and drove to the nearby shop, where I stocked up with goodies for the tea. As she munched her meal, full of praise for our generosity at such short notice, she was unaware that she was eating her own money!

We rehearsed a new music hall show during the last few weeks of *The Good Old Days*, and this was another long runner. Featured in both shows was the late Mickser Reid, who was always used by Cecil when possible. Mickser was a dwarf, of great spirit, and an accomplished acrobat.

Later on, when poor Mickser died, someone was commiserating with Cecil on his loss a day or two before the funeral. 'Where are you going now?' he asked Cecil with annoying inquisitiveness.

Cecil's reply was sharp, and to the point: 'Up to McGuire and Patterson's to buy him a coffin.' (McGuire and Patterson supplied Ireland with boxes of matches.)

When the second music hall show ended, I was quite seriously out of work, but 'keeping my cool'. We were having lunch one Sunday when the phone rang. It was the late Seamus Forde, of Radio Éireann, asking me to write for and perform in a radio show, featuring comedian Hal Roach. I agreed on the spot, and returned to the lunch table, glowing. Bairbre and the children had only digested the news when the phone rang again.

It was Jack Cruise, who wanted me to join his show as his 'feed' on tour in Cork and Limerick. The money was forty pounds a week. This seemed like a fortune at the time, and I jumped at it. After I had put the phone down it dawned on me that the dates of the two shows coincided. I was so full of energy, and so hungry for money, success and work that I decided to do the two shows.

This entailed arriving at Radio Éireann, in Henry Street, in Dublin, at 10 a.m. sharp, and writing a sketch or two with some other scriptwriters. At 3 p.m., I would down tools, saying that inspiration had dried up as far as I was concerned. Seamus accepted this, as he realised that a sketch a day wasn't a bad output. I would then jump into the car and drive to Cork, arriving there at about ten minutes to eight, just in time for the show at the Cork Opera House, and then drive back to Dublin after the show.

I did this six days a week for two weeks, in Cork and Limerick, where we appeared in the old Savoy Theatre. Food was grabbed at lunch hour in the Radio Éireann canteen, and various 'greasy spoons' in places like Urlingford and Cashel. It was the hardest stint I ever did, and I don't think I could do it again. I know that I put an amazing mileage total on the clock of my poor car.

It was all worth it, though. Just imagine: from ten pounds a week to a total of seventy pounds! It seemed like gold bars, and it started a working relationship with Jack Cruise, which lasted for four years, entailing summer shows and pantos, with time in between for plays. Cruise also used to take his company on 'run-outs'. These were one-off variety shows down the country, returning the same night: tough work, but great fun.

During this period, a most innovative and productive company came into being at the Eblana. It was called 'Amalgamated Artists', and mounted most adventurous plays, like Orton's *Loot* and *What the Butler Saw*, Peter Nichols' *A Day in the Death of Joe Egg*, and Kevin Laffan's *It's a Two Feet Six Inches Above the Ground World*.

The chief play reader was actor Des Nealon, who should be asked by other companies to supply this service today. He has the best nose for spotting a good play that I have ever encountered. In *It's a Two Feet Six Inches Above the Ground World*, I had the pleasure of playing a caretaker, named Baker, who is wrongly accused of showing his privates to a small boy, and who invades the home of his little accuser, and refuses to leave.

The child's father is a sanctimonious prat, who refuses to take into account the fact that his long-suffering wife doesn't wish to bear a child a year, and is advised by a very interfering and conservative priest friend, who is almost a 'live-in' spiritual counsellor. The arguments over the merits of artificial birth control between the priest, the husband and wife, and Baker, are some of the best comedy scenes I have encountered.

At one time the caretaker lists nine or ten very coarse expressions for the act of sexual intercourse, and the priest intervenes with: 'making love is sufficient.' All the caretaker had to do to get a huge laugh was to nod in assent, as if to say: 'Yeah, that's another one! Why didn't I think of that?'

I had a get-out clause in this production, because I had a prior engagement, but I was to find myself back in the same role in the Olympia Theatre, with a different cast, after a Jack Cruise show. Somehow the intimacy of the Eblana was more suited to the show, and it never went as well in the Olympia. However, I have experienced high drama, both on and off stage in the Olympia. I was in one play where the heroine was in mid-speech onstage, when two Gardaí appeared in the wings, asking me about her identity.

I had no choice but to confirm it. They asked me to tell her that they wanted to interview her immediately, but I told them that if they wanted to do that, they would have to walk onstage themselves.

They both began to blush, saying that I was much more qualified to walk onstage than they. However, I was adamant. If they wanted to question her, they would have to walk on the stage there and then. There was no way that I was going to interrupt a major production before a packed house. They said that they would be too shy so I told them that they would have to wait for the final curtain.

When we had all taken our bows, I turned to tell the heroine that the Gardaí were waiting to question her, but she had vapourised. There was just no trace of her. The Gardaí and I searched the theatre high and low, but without success. The set was a two-level affair, with a big double bed on the upper floor. As a last resort, the two officers mounted the stairs and went aloft.

There was still no sign of her. The bed clothes were completely flat, but as a last hopeless gesture, the boys pulled the clothes back, and there she was. I never knew that anyone could make themselves so flat, and she was not unendowed by nature!

The alleged crime necessitated her being brought to the Bridewell Garda Station, on the North Quays, and I had to accompany her. For some reason the rest of the company were unaware of this. They had all gone to the bar. I think I had been hypnotised by the gravitas of the Gardaí, and overzealous in helping them.

When we arrived at the Bridewell it was like an episode from *Hill Street Blues*. There were drunks, junkies, arrest-resistors, and ladies of the night all over the place.

They were having a busy night. I didn't know that such a world existed in Dublin. It was chaos. The Gardaí wanted five hundred pounds bail from me, and were very insistent, but I told them that the best I could do was an assurance of fifty pounds. Right in the middle of the negotiations, a young Garda burst in through the doors, blood pouring frighteningly from a head wound down the front of his uniform. He was soaked to the waist. Nobody paid much heed to the poor young man.

After some time they caved in, and settled for the fifty pound assurance. I phoned Bairbre and told her where I was, and it sounded so outrageous that she believed me. By this time it was 2 a.m. I thought that I had seen it all until I looked into the hallway, where a huge conga of Garda personnel was making its noisy way up the stairs, male and female Gardaí, all in their civilian clothes, with paper hats on their heads. God knows, they had the right to celebrate if they wanted to, but it made a bizarre spectacle.

Allegations had been made about some considerable financial irregularity with cheques, but what it was I will never know. The case never came up for hearing and the actress departed to England at the end of the run. I was never asked to fork out the fifty pounds.

18

The Gay Issue
and the Theatre of the Absurd

The rights of the gay community were only beginning to be seriously discussed when I was offered the part of Emory in a play called *The Boys in the Band*, written by Mart Crowley. It was a most moving depiction of the social isolation of the gay community in New York. Nowadays it wouldn't have the same impact. Things have moved on, and there is much greater recognition of the rights of gay people.

The play was highly emotive, and it is a great credit to the Dublin audiences that never once was there a heckle, a kissing sound or a boo throughout its run. It ran for one month, with matinees, and there was never an empty seat. The plot centred around a very cruel game, in which each guest at a party had to tell the story of his greatest love; to strip himself bare emotionally.

It was brutal, but really educated the audience about another way of life. Indeed, so moving was that part of the show that an old lady burst out crying one night and had to be led out sobbing, saying: 'This is very moving, really very moving!'

Some members of the cast were gay, and very funny and witty. Actors did the odd bold thing onstage, mainly led by the director, John Carlyle, who would change his timing now and then, just to keep you on your toes. He had been particularly annoying to me one night when I decided to get my revenge.

There was a scene where I had to serve the cast with helpings of lasagne. They all queued up and I dished it out. Carlyle had to say: 'I'm going to have seconds, and I'm going to have thirds, and I'm going to have a fat attack!'

He had to consume his portion after this, and then present himself for another plateful on cue, before speaking again. I had given him a huge portion to finish in the time. As he presented himself for his second portion, his eyes bulging from having swallowed the first portion, he was faced with another huge one. Horror-stricken, he muttered abuse at me under his heavily garlic-laced breath.

We had one black actor in the play, named Rudy Patterson. He was a lovely guy, gentle and relaxed, so gentle in fact, that one night he actually fell asleep onstage. I had never believed that such a thing could happen, although more of that anon. There was nothing the stage management could do to help. He was out of their reach. The writing was slick and funny, and at one stage he was referred to as 'The African Queen'.

My friend, Emmet Bergin, gave a fine performance, playing against type as a kind of Jon Voight character, named 'Cowboy', who is given as a birthday present to one of the guests. No one could be 'straighter' than Emmet, but he made a great job of it.

Actors can be very dependent on the stage manager and the assistant stage manager to come to their aid in times of crisis. The best example is the 'prompt', when someone has 'dried'. There are few things more traumatising than when your mind goes completely blank onstage. If there isn't a quick recovery, the whole illusion of the characterisation is lost. Prompts must be clear, even at the expense of being heard by the audience.

I was once appearing in the Eblana, in an absurdist play, written by a charming ex-naval man named Harry Barton. It was extremely opaque, and the text was very difficult to learn, because there were no clear images to mark any turning points, and it was almost impossible to hang one sentence on another.

It is hard to memorise anything which doesn't have any apparent structure. I dried, and waited patiently for a prompt. I could hear the frantic turning of pages of the prompt copy of the play in the stage left corner, indicating, unforgivably, that it hadn't been open at the correct page. This was followed by a loud hiss of: 'But if?'

I had never had a more useless prompt in my life. I strode offstage and grabbed the prompt copy, saying quite loudly: 'But if fucking what?' and strode back on to the stage, resuming the speech. The play was so incomprehensible that the audience must have thought that it was part of the action, because there was no indication on their part that they thought that anything was amiss.

Improvisation can reach ludicrous heights when stage management is faced with a challenge. In one play at the Gate, there was a cue for a phone to ring offstage at a critical moment, and when it arrived, there was a frantic clicking sound from the battery-powered device which simulates a phone ringing.

The cast waited patiently, and eventually heard running feet headed for the other side of the stage, where there was another similar device. There was more frantic clicking, then a pause, followed by a loud actorish voice saying: 'Driiiiiiinnnng, driiiiiiinnnng, driiiiiiinnnng, driiiiiiinnnng!'

I spent six years altogether working at the Gate Theatre with the Edwards MacLiammóir Company, and although we all groaned at the annual utterances of Hilton Edwards, at the beginning of each season, on reflection, they were unfailingly correct.

One was: 'If you are going at a pace that suits yourself, you can bet your bottom dollar that you are boring the balls off your audience.' Nothing could be truer. (Church preachers please take note!) It is the job of a good raconteur, preacher or actor, to 'lead' their audience. He or she must be at least half a beat ahead of them.

Theatre audiences don't pay good money to know exactly what's coming next. There isn't much excitement in knowing exactly what a character is going to say next, is there?

Hilton had many other adages, including: 'Just remember that the theatre is a temple. The audience comes to worship, and you are the minister. If you lose that relationship, you have lost the audience.'

I remember when a young actor questioned one of Hilton's directions one day, in a somewhat arrogant manner. Hilton heard him out with mock respect. When the actor had finished his question, Hilton transfixed him with a laser-like gaze, saying: 'Yes, you could do it like that alright, dear boy, but then you might be left with ego all over your face.'

Hilton was of the 'old school' of directors. He directed, and with honourable exceptions, you did what he said. On one occasion he was directing two young actors, of the new school, in a Broadway play, in New York. They wanted to discuss what they had had for their breakfasts, whether they had been breast-fed, their bowel movements and anything else which might reveal the sub-text of the play.

Hilton listened patiently for a couple of hours, and then said: 'Look, you two chaps, I so admire the way you young fellows work nowadays, exploring all these possible extensions of the meaning of the play, so I have a suggestion: I think we should break for today, and perhaps you two chaps might meet for dinner this evening and discuss all these things, and then we'll meet here at 9 a.m. tomorrow morning, and we'll fucking do it my way!'

Apropos of the Stanislavski school of acting – in which there is so much that is good – an American actor, named Philip O'Brien, was waiting offstage to say his entry lines, and every time he stepped on the set, the director stopped him with some query or suggestion. Now Philip was not the kind of actor who would lightly dismiss useful sub-textual suggestions, but he was weary of this director's ability to waste time.

The director stopped him on about his third attempt to enter onstage, with, 'Philip, what are you thinking?'

Philip replied, 'I'm thinking that this play opens Monday night at eight, and if I don't get to say these lines, maybe we won't open at all.'

The director said, 'No, Philip. I mean, what is your character thinking?'

Philip said, 'Leave it with me,' and stepped offstage.

He was back in ten seconds or so, with, 'He agrees with me!'

Returning to Hilton, on the morning after Bloody Sunday in Derry, we were all assembled in the green room in the Gate, waiting to begin rehearsal. Hilton just sat there, staring into space, with a copy of the *Irish Times* on his knee. Then he stirred himself out of his reverie. Pointing to the horrific headlines, he said, sadly, 'Today, I am ashamed to be an Englishman.'

The Gate provided great continuity of work, and a very pleasant company. Hilton was a master of lighting design. His scenes looked like a series of Tintorettos. There was no one who could use colours like Hilton, and I don't think that there has been a lighting designer to touch him since. He was also a master when it came to directing crowd scenes. As Lennox Robinson once said of him: 'Hilton can take two people, and make them look like three!'

19

The Importance of Being Micheál, and the Power of Being Deaf

Micheál MacLiammóir was a truly amazing man, multi-talented, and very kind to beginners. He was a true Renaissance man. His accomplishment included costume design, playwriting, playing the piano, painting, and a comprehensive knowledge of the French and Irish languages. He had a fair knowledge of many other languages as well.

One day, we were rehearsing a play when someone noticed that Micheál's edition of the script was different to the one which we were all using. He was reading from an old leather-bound volume. A cast member made his way quietly behind Micheál, and found that he was working from a French text of the play with complete facility, uttering all his lines in English in his rich Irish brogue.

He was unfailingly kind to me, although we didn't get off to the best of starts. My first meeting with him was in the wardrobe department of the Gaiety Theatre, during *Saint Joan of the Stockyards*, where he was having a spectacular row with Hilton. They used to relish their public rows, spurring each other on to the most extravagant imagery in their abuse. Eventually there was a lull, and Micheál called me over to him, and pointing to Hilton, said: 'Go over and tell that man that I am not speaking to him!'

It was a horrible job, but I had to go over to Hilton and say to him: 'Excuse me Mr Edwards, but Dr MacLiammóir says that he is not speaking to you.' I had never felt like such a lackey in my life.

But later Micheál and I became quite friendly. He always took time with me, and it was a pleasure to talk to him. There was always something to learn. Conversation was always about something of substance. He had no time for small talk. On one occasion, when I played a role in *The Lads*, Joe O'Donnell's play, directed by Alan Simpson of *The Rose Tattoo* fame, Micheál sneaked into the back of the theatre. At one stage I had to do press-ups, while wearing bright red underpants. Micheál slipped away into the night afterwards, avoiding the pilgrimage backstage.

The play was all about 'laddishness' and flat life in Dublin, not Micheál's cup of tea at all, with its avowed heterosexuality and bad language. Some time later he wrote me a letter, saying that the play hadn't been to his taste. However, he said that red was his favourite colour in underpants, and he always wore red ones himself. I still have the letter. He was a worthy inheritor of the mantle of Oscar Wilde.

The years in the Gate threw up its fair share of eccentrics. One was an actor named Reggie Jarman, a profoundly deaf old actor, who wore a hearing aid which was as big as a small portable radio, and which used to utter loud squeaks now and then. It must have been one of the first hearing aids available commercially. When it squeaked, Reggie would mutter an apology and twiddle a little knob on the side of it. This device lived in his left breast pocket.

He was an avid cricket fan, and for long periods would switch off the hearing aid, and plug a little lead into his ear from a radio which he kept in his right inner pocket. When this happened you had no chance whatsoever of contact with him. At rehearsal, when Hilton could get no reaction from him, he would shout at him in a loud voice: 'Reggie, are you switched on or switched off?'

There would be a flurry of action from Reggie, and after a loud squeak from the hearing aid, he would say: 'Switched on, Hilton, switched on!'

When you were onstage with Reggie, he lip-read you, and thus, when you faced away from him, all contact was lost. Apart from Rudy, in *The Boys in the Band* he was the only other actor I knew who fell asleep on the stage.

Thus in a production of Desmond Forristal's *The True Story of the Horrid Popish Plot*, when the curtain rose, Reggie, who was playing the part of Horrocks, the famous hanging judge, was already fast asleep. The plot revolved around the trial of Oliver Plunkett for treason, on the evidence of the great perjurer, Titus Oates, and the curtain rose on the court scene, with all the lords assembled on either side of the judge, and at either side of the stage, in witness boxes, Oliver Plunkett and Titus Oates.

I was playing the role of Titus Oates, and was just about to give my perjured evidence, when Reggie awoke suddenly, with: 'Prisoner at the Bar, you have been found guilty of treasonable activity against our great King Charles. You are hereby sentenced to be taken from this court, and to be drawn upon a hurdle to Tyburn, where your bowels shall be cut out and shown to you, and then burned before your eyes, and then you shall be hanged, drawn and quartered.'

These were the final lines of the play, and there was now no need for the audience to sit for another hour and a quarter. Christopher Casson, seasoned pro that he was, rose from his seat, and gathering his voluminous cloak around him, while holding on to his great floppy velvet hat, moved as though on wheels up to the judge, and muttered in his ear.

Reggie brushed him aside with: 'Oh very well then, let the trial proceed if you must!' And the play was salvaged. It was always rumoured that Hilton employed Reggie because he was eternally grateful to him for stealing Hilton's fiancée away from him and marrying her, thus leaving him free to follow his true sexual orientation.

Reggie was an incurable gambler, and was reputed to have gone through his wife's fortune, as well as a few of his own. I didn't believe this until one day he asked me where he could find 'a good game of poker' in Dublin. Now, people who ask that question are usually heavy gamblers. I told him that I didn't know of one, and asked him whether he played for high stakes.

'Ah, my dear boy,' he replied sadly, 'if you only knew the fortunes I have won and lost.' There was a kind of sad wistfulness in his words, and later, when there was a short break in rehearsal, he was allowed to go over to London to see his wife. When he returned he showed me a truly prodigious bank roll. I expressed appropriate wonder, and he said: 'I expect that it will be gone very soon.' Once again I was left with the impression of considerable sadness.

20

Invasion

The Gate Theatre seemed to lend itself to strange theatrical happenings. In a production of Anouilh's *Time Remembered*, mounted by the doughty Phyllis Ryan, of Gemini Productions, there was a requirement for a gypsy orchestra, but unfortunately the company's finances didn't run to a full orchestra. This constituted quite a problem. What to do? Then the solution dawned on Phyllis (who always fought my corner loyally). She knew that I played the violin, and I was approached to become a one-man gypsy orchestra. Quite an undertaking!

I received an extra seven pounds a week for this honour, of doubling as orchestra and actor. It transpired that Phyllis had fought tooth and nail to get me an extra seven pounds a week, against an investor, who later turned out to have been my former agent. Some agent!

The play was rehearsed, and opened in all its glory. The plot consists largely of a conversation at a café table between two lovers, with the gypsy orchestra playing passionately in the background, and later in the garden. It eventually transpires that the man is a prince. As the couple sweep on to the stage, the lady throws a rose to the orchestra.

I was playing Monti's 'Czardas' with all the gusto I could muster, when the rose twirled through the air, and landed prickly stalk side down, right between the strings of the violin, just at the bridge. I ground to a halt, with some alarming squawks, and then had to extract the stem with some difficulty. The emotion-laden reminiscences of the lovers got off to a shaky start.

The play settled down nicely, and was drawing reasonably good audiences, when another bizarre event occurred.

One night I was dusting down tables, waiting for an order from the Prince, when a very drunken American lurched towards the stage apron, saying: 'Any chance of getting a drink round here?' in a very loud voice.

He clambered up on to the stage, and staggered towards me, saying: 'C'mon, gimme a beer! I wanna beer!' Plonking himself down in a chair, he said: 'Isn't there any goddam service around here?' The lady and the Prince just froze.

I tried to incorporate the Yank into the play by frantic, bad, improvisation, but to no avail. He was becoming more and more aggressive. Suddenly my dilemma was resolved. The stage carpenter, Kevin Hutson, a man of fine physique, strode onstage, and taking the drunk by his shoulder and elbow, whipped him out of his seat, and said: 'I am afraid you are in the wrong place sir,' and marched him swiftly off the stage.

Aptly, the next line in the script was, 'Well then. Where were we?'

This was interpreted by the audience as the greatest display of self-possession they had ever seen, and was greeted by thunderous and prolonged applause.

I have to acknowledge the debt I owe to Phyllis Ryan for her belief in me as a young actor. Every actor has criticisms to make of producers for one reason or another, some of them well founded, and some of them sour grapes. None of us is without fault, actors, directors and producers, but Phyllis always employed me when she could, and encouraged me. To be believed in when you are young is a great boon, and I must thank Phyllis for her support over the years.

Phyllis, Anna Manahan and I toured for three and a half years around the country with two productions, *Matchmaker*, Ray

McAnally's skilful adaptation of the letters of John B. Keane, and Eric Cross's *The Tailor and Ansty*. We survived without any major falling-out between us, and it kept us in a crust when very little was happening for us.

Initially, Anna was the most solvent of the three of us. She had put a little away from her stint in *Memoirs of an Irish R.M.*, although she had put a good hole in this by buying her house. Her generosity was unfailing. At the start of each tour, Phyllis and I had to borrow a 'float' each from Anna, because we were very short of cash at the time. This would be repaid at the end of the first week. I don't think we would have been able to survive those tours without Anna's generosity. We travelled in my specimen Cortina car, a 1963 series three, which, being over the age of twenty, was hardly the kind of vehicle for such excessive extra mileage, but it stood the test, although it was a terrible thing to do to such a collector's item. Scandalised car buffs used to say to me round the country: 'You're not actually using that car as your "road car", are you?'

We played in improvised theatres in hotels, village halls, and most of the main theatres in rural Ireland, travelling in all weather conditions. The driving was quite exhausting, and I felt somewhat isolated as Phyllis and Anna lapsed into conversation for long periods, on subjects to which I could make no contribution. It is easy to miss a critical signpost on leaving a busy provincial town, and I was wearied by navigation, trying to watch out for other cars and lorries, while keeping on the lookout for road signs. Anna and Phyllis were in deep conversation, which I interrupted with: 'Excuse me ladies, but I would appreciate it if you could keep an eye out for road signs as we leave towns. It's difficult to negotiate your way between lorries and cars, and read road signs at the same time.'

Due notice was taken of this, and some time later, Anna interrupted her narrative with: 'Fresh Eggs!' Her cry had been an instinctive, if literal, reaction to my injunction. It was tough graft, but I have happy memories of that constant touring.

$-\!\!\!\sim\!\!\!-$ **21** $-\!\!\!\sim\!\!\!-$

Misunderstanding, and a Loveable Rogue

One major Phyllis Ryan production which I played in was a Dublin Theatre Festival production of Hugh Leonard's *The Patrick Pearse Motel*, in the Olympia Theatre, with John Gregson, May Cluskey, Rosaleen Linehan, and Angela Vale. It was directed by James Grout, who appeared in many British TV series and films.

I played the role of a brash, cheeky entrepreneur, who was always trying to keep up with the older, and established business mogul, played by the late Godfrey Quigley. The play was a send-up of the modern, consumer-driven Ireland which was emerging at the time. It was really prophetic, because looking at the Ireland we live in now, nature would appear to be following art.

Godfrey and James Grout and Hugh Leonard would lunch together during the rehearsal period, and the play would be discussed. One day, they returned from lunch, and rehearsal recommenced. We were just a few minutes into a scene between Godfrey and myself, when Godfrey announced to me that he had a new Jensen car. This wasn't in the script, but I immediately fell back on the Variety technique, which abhors a vacuum.

'Oh great,' I enthused. 'Will you let me drive her? I'd love to try her out!'

Godfrey became apoplectic. 'What is this boy saying to me? This isn't in the script. What is this boy saying to me?'

'Well,' I replied, 'your bloody line wasn't in the script either.'

James Grout, a man of some bulk, came running from the back of the theatre to try and restore the peace between us. It transpired that the line had been thought up over lunch, and Godfrey seemed to think that I should have known this by some form of telepathy. We continued with the rehearsal, but relations between me and Godfrey remained frosty after that.

During the run, Godfrey broke his leg while crossing the road near where he lived. The management was in a state of high fever. Would the show have to close? Hugh Leonard offered to play the part himself, but Godfrey, real trouper that he was, insisted in going onstage on crutches. He succeeded in doing this by seating himself in strategic places onstage for the longer speeches. It didn't affect the bookings in the least, and we continued to play to packed houses.

Godfrey had a very soft side to him. He could become extremely emotional at the drop of a hat. There was a part of the play where he needed to produce a handkerchief, and one night, just before he was due to make his entrance on crutches, he discovered, to his horror, that he was without the handkerchief. There was no getting upstairs to the dressing room in time. He was in a panic.

For some reason, which I can't remember, I carried a beautiful white linen handkerchief in my pocket throughout the play. It wasn't in my breast pocket, so it may just have been some neurosis. I whipped out the handkerchief and presented it to Godfrey, who was so overcome by his delivery from doom that he burst out crying. We dried his eyes with tissues and got him onstage. Afterwards he thanked me profusely, and I knew there and then that good relations had been restored. We were always friendly to each other after that.

The late John Gregson was a loveable mess of a character, with an amazing fund of tales about films in which he had appeared. He really had been a matinee idol, mobbed by women wherever he went. His air of vulnerability and good looks made nearly every woman he met want to jump into bed with him. He was seated in the bar in the Wicklow Hotel in Dublin one day, when a woman who was a complete stranger to him, turned around suddenly and bit him in the arm through his shirt sleeve.

When he asked her why she had done this, she replied that she had wanted to bite him for years. When I looked incredulous, he rolled up his sleeve and showed me the marks, which were really impressive. There was no mistaking the classic pattern.

John had some great stories about the ups and downs of his career. At one stage, when he was at a very low ebb, he wandered around to the home of a neighbour on the Thames bank in search of company. There was no reply to his ring on the bell, so having a key, he let himself in to await his friend's return. He was sprawled in an armchair when there was a ring on the doorbell.

When he opened the door, there was a group of gentlemen there who told him that they were considering the house as the location for a TV commercial for Hamlet cigars. John took them on the grand tour, and they said that the house would be ideal, so he made a deal with them there and then to let the house to them for a very handsome fee. They couldn't believe their luck in meeting 'the' John Gregson, and asked him whether he would lower himself to do a cigar commercial.

John said that he might consider it if they got in touch with his agent. They were in the middle of this conversation when the owner of the house returned home. John took him firmly by the elbow, and 'told' him that he was letting his house for the filming of a commercial whether he liked it or not. John would split the proceeds of the rental with him, but they would have to pretend that it was John's house. The bewildered man agreed, and John warned his agent of the impending call, and got himself a handsome fee.

Later that week the company took over the house and made a complete mess of it for a couple of days, but the owner was quite pleased with his portion of the rent. Many readers will remember that Hamlet commercial, which is now considered to be a classic.

John had been having a fairly rough time when he came over to do the play. He wasn't awash with money. I loved his frankness about his career. He had done it all; earned fortunes, and spent nail-biting periods out of work. He didn't go in for coy terms like 'resting'. He had a get-out clause with the management, should a certain job come up.

When the call came to go over to London for an interview with Shirley MacLaine for a part in a series about life in a newspaper office, the problem was that John had very little money. I offered him a loan, which he was happy to accept. So, off he flew, early one morning, to meet Ms MacLaine in London. Being the shambles he was, he had no decent tie to wear, so I gave him a loan of one of mine. I was intensely proud of being in a position to help a 'real movie star'.

He couldn't find his trouser belt on the morning of his departure, so he used my tie to hold up his trousers. Just before his interview with Ms MacLaine, he put on the tie, and held up his trousers by putting his hands in his pockets, but introductions became difficult when it came to the hand-shaking stage. One of Ms MacLaine's aides asked why he kept his hands in his pockets, and he had to confess that if he took them out his trousers would fall down. He sat down listening to the scornful laughter of the aides, but he turned the tables on them.

He asked Ms MacLaine had she eaten, and when she told him that she had eaten nothing since early morning, he said: 'Is this the way they treat you? Do you allow them to treat you like this?'

She responded beautifully by berating her aides for neglecting her so badly, and John swept her off to lunch on my money. By the time they parted, the job was his. He arrived back from Dublin Airport half an hour before the show, and we celebrated his success in the bar that night. When he left the show, he was replaced by Norman Rodway, who was also terrific in the part, and John, true gentleman that he was, repaid his debt to me.

22

The Great John McIvor

My next encounter with a Hugh Leonard play was with his autobiographical *Da*, again produced by Gemini Production's. I played the role of Oliver, the hero's boyhood friend. The show starred John McIvor, an American actor, as Da. Also starring were Kevin McHugh, as Charlie Now, Chris O'Neill as Charlie Then, and Dearbhla Molloy as The Yellow Peril. It was directed by another American, Jim Waring, who had directed a performance of it for Hugh Leonard in the US.

McIvor will be remembered for his performance in *Midnight Cowboy*, as the pervert with all the religious emblems in his room, complete with flashing lights, which proved too daunting even for Jon Voight's character. Of course he played in many other films as well, such as *Breakfast at Tiffany's* and *The Manchurian Candidate*.

He was very droll and encouraging. I had a line which I used to milk for an exit round of applause. It occurs when the two young lads, Charlie and his priggish friend, Oliver, are gazing at the young girl, the Yellow Peril, down Dún Laoghaire pier. There is a difference of opinion between the two lads about their intentions towards the girl, and Oliver, shocked by Charlie's lust, says: 'Well don't salute me when you see me again on the pier, because you won't be saluted back!' I used to milk this prissy outburst for all it was worth, and it always got a round. As I came offstage each night, McIvor would be waiting in the wings to make his entrance.

He would say: 'That's it! Good boy! Get your clack. Good boy!' He had been around long enough to know that you are on your own when it comes to getting a legitimate laugh. There are always some people in the theatre who feel that laughter is a 'cheap' reaction in a play which is not basically a comedy, but John McIvor wouldn't have hunted with them.

One day myself and Chris O'Neill were rehearsing the Yellow Peril scene with Jim Waring. The whole point of the scene is the atmosphere of sexual repression which prevailed in Ireland at that time. The two boys would talk suggestively about The Yellow Peril, but it would always be mere talk. Most people of my age remember the false bravado of their early sex talk.

We were discussing the scene when Jim Waring said: 'You two guys are what, fourteen or so? Hell, you guys would have lost your virginity by now, wouldn't you?'

Chris and I looked at him in amazement.

'Oh, not in Ireland we wouldn't,' we chorused. Jim just shrugged his shoulders wearily, and said: 'I'll leave you two guys to work this out, and when I come back we'll go with whatever you decide.' The cultural divide was just too great for him.

McIvor had tremendous 'presence' onstage. He could dominate any scene. There was a sense of latent dramatic power within him. You felt that all he had to do was twitch, and the scene was his, although he was most generous onstage. If the scene was yours, he would never steal the attention.

One day at rehearsals, Jim said to him: 'Hey John, while you're up there at the kitchen press, you can be fixing a drink for yourself or something.'

McIvor turned his impressive bulk in Jim's direction. And looked at him with huge kindly eyes. 'Jim,' he said, 'I'm acting my goddam ass off!' Suddenly we realised the power of the man. He could have destroyed all of us by raising an eyebrow.

The show went on tour afterwards to Limerick and Cork, with Eddie Golden as Da, and was highly successful. I was asked to drive no less than five other actors from Limerick to Cork. The car was a Ford Corsair, designed to hold five adults. Now six adults in a car is a crowd. But add their luggage and you are carrying a fair weight.

When we got to Cork we had to stop on Patrick's Hill, which has an alarmingly steep gradient, to allow some of the actors to disembark with their luggage. I got out of the car to remove their luggage, leaving the car in first gear with the handbrake pulled tight. Suddenly the car began to leapfrog backwards, defying brake and gearbox. I tried to jump into the driver's seat, but to no avail, and watched helplessly as my car ploughed into the one behind.

The driver was a courtly, elderly gentleman, accompanied by his wife. When I presented myself at his car he was cool and rational, unlike so many who might have been overtaken by road rage. I felt that I just couldn't face an insurance hassle, and I decided to risk all.

It transpired that the man lived in an apartment near Victoria Terrace, nearby. Now, my own digs were in Victoria Terrace. I asked the man would he trust me to replace the light fitting which my car had crushed myself, the following morning, explaining that it would be easy to find me if I defaulted, because I would be staying right beside him, and would be playing for a week at the Opera House. The dear man trusted me.

The following morning I rose early and walked down over the bridge across the River Lee to a huge motor parts dealership, where I found exactly the part I wanted, and headed back to the other side of the river to where his car was parked outside his apartment.

Fixing the light was easy, because it was held in position by a sprung mechanism. I clawed out the broken headlight with the aid of tools which I had brought with me, and having shoved in the plug pushed the new light home. You would never have known that the car had been in an accident. When I left, there was no one around, and only my footprints in the morning frost, so obviously when the owner came out to look at his car, he found that a miracle had been performed.

All that week I was being accosted in Cork city, with: 'I hear you're a man of your word. You fixed a headlight for a friend of mine. Is it the Opera House you're appearing in?' I had unwittingly bought us a fund of goodwill. But that's Cork. Word travels quickly there.

— 23 —

A National Institution

I was never in the bosom of the Abbey Theatre, although I have played there a few times in the course of my jobbing career as an actor. The Abbey is, of course, a national institution, and its function and place in the national artistic life is always a matter of heated, and often bitter, debate. I have never had any very strong feelings about the matter, or felt entitled to comment, because I haven't had any ongoing association with the Abbey, and thus, no vested interested in it as a performer.

I would probably have strong opinions if I were a director or a playwright, rather than a roving player, and someone who has always worked on a number of performing fronts. Many of the people whom I have encountered, who have devoted their entire careers to the Abbey, command my profound respect. In fact, I often experience a sense of inferiority when I hear them discussing theatre, because my own theatrical education is so full of holes.

However, fate dealt the cards, and the opportunities which came my way to keep my family fed shaped me as I am. It was impossible to get into the Abbey when I started out. There were no interviews going at the time. The theatre was very set in its ways, and it must be said, very cut off from the general theatre. Abbey players were a caste apart, and although great company socially, as a general rule they didn't go to see what was going on in other theatres. Also, a fluency in the Irish language was a 'must'. There has been a vast change since the days of Ernest Blythe.

My first realisation that the Abbey was a world unto itself was when I presented myself for a rehearsal in Dublin for my first engagement there. I had a high profile on television at the time, being thrust into people's faces as much as three times a week. For good or ill, one gets known to the public, and this leads to the usual catcalling on the streets and in buses. It is one of the hazards of being on television.

I boarded a bus from Monkstown to the city and was subjected to catcalls all the way into town by schoolgoers. I played a wide variety of characters at the time, and was called by their various names, as well as my own.

When I reached town I thought I could lose myself in the crowd, but spotters will spot. I was hailed constantly, this time being called mostly by my own name.

I scuttled from O'Connell Street down Lower Abbey Street, where I was surrounded by a good-humoured circle of taxi drivers. Many of them shadow-boxed with me, which I found reassuring, because I used to train in a popular gym, as did many of them, and this was a friendly acknowledgement of a joint interest. I went on my way reassured to the Abbey stage door, where I encountered the doorman, the late Al Kohler, who threw the door open and received me with: 'Welcome to the Abbey, Mr Ryan!'

In that chastening moment, I realised that if you thought that you had a profile outside the Abbey, you certainly hadn't one inside. I told this tale one time on a TV chat show, and a columnist in the *Sunday Independent* interpreted it as egotistical shock on my part that I hadn't been recognised, thus missing the whole point of the story. The point was, that at that time, the Abbey had its own set of priorities, and paid little attention to exposure on the other media.

It was Tomás Mac Anna who had asked me to be in the play, and I was very pleased that he had made it possible for me to pass through the sacred portals. The play we were doing was *The Far-*

Off Hills, by Lennox Robinson. It was a pleasure to work in the National Theatre for the first time. Rehearsals went well, and Tomás was most supportive throughout.

I played the role of Patrick Clancy, a blind man. There is a scene in the play where a love affair had developed between Patrick and Susie Tynan, who was played by Kathleen Barrington, and where Susie takes the initiative in kissing Patrick. Such moments have to be handled with great delicacy onstage. Any slip can cause a snigger, and convincing acting is a 'must'.

Kathleen had handled the lovemaking beautifully, and we had the rapt attention of the entire audience when an American lady tourist theatregoer in the front row (the Americans always arrived in huge tourist coaches from the hotels), suddenly projectile-vomited all over the front of the stage. We held the kiss during the consternation which followed, waiting for it to subside, but she performed again, this time all over the front row, and once again on the way out.

I don't think that Lennox Robinson ever envisaged such a long and passionate kiss, particularly at the time when the play was written. As we detached lips, I whispered into Kathleen's ear: 'I hope to God it wasn't the acting!'

$-\sim\!\!\sim\!\!-$ 24 $-\sim\!\!\sim\!\!-$

Blind Balladeer

Tomás Mac Anna directed me in a musical in the Olympia Theatre, called *My Name is Zozimus*, about a famous eighteenth-century Dublin street rhymer. The show featured The Wolfe Tones, giving their fine renditions of the verses of the balladeer, and I was playing the role of the balladeer himself. It was a big, demanding role, but there was little satisfaction in it for me, because The Wolfe Tones performed the songs, which logically should have been performed by Zozimus himself, and somehow the format didn't work.

It was such a pity, because the story of Zozimus is such an interesting one. He was born in 1794 in Faddle Alley, which was situated in the Liberties, off the now vanished Ducker's Lane, a passage between Blackpitts and Clanbrassil Street. His real name was Michael Moran, and although born with sight, he was stricken by illness and became blind when he was a fortnight old.

In spite of his disability and the extreme poverty of his parents, by the use of his extraordinary memory and the power of his voice, he was able to support himself and his family as a renowned street rhymer and performer of ballads, poems and essays.

He wore a long, coarse, dark frieze coat with a cape, which was so ragged at the hemline that it appeared to be scalloped. His hat was a beaver one, brown and greasy, and on his feet he wore a pair of sturdy Francis Street brogues. Secured to his wrist by a leather thong, was a large blackthorn staff, with an iron ferrule sat at the end.

Come evening time, he would set out on his route, Carlisle, Wood Quay, Church Street and Bloody Bridges; up and down Dame Street, Capel Street and Sackville Street, Grafton Street, Henry Street and the Conciliation Hall. When he arrived at his place of performance, he would proclaim:

> Ye sons and daughters of Ireland attend,
> Gather round poor Zozimus your friend,
> Listen boys until ye hear,
> My charming song so dear.

Then he would entrust himself to the goodwill of his faithful followers, saying: 'Boys, am I standin' in a puddle? Am I standin' in the wet?' One of his favourite ballads was 'The Finding Of Moses':

> In Egypt's land, contagious to the Nile,
> Pharoah's daughter went to bathe herself in style,
> She tuk her dip, then went unto the land,
> And for to dry her royal pelt,
> She ran along the strand,
> A bulrush tripped her, whereupon she saw,
> A smilin' little babby in a wad of straw,
> She picked the babby up, and said in accents wild,
> Thunderin' ages girls, which wan o'yez owns this child?

Zozimus discovered his vocation when he was 'nine and a quarter years old', on 20 September 1803, the day Robert Emmet was hanged in Thomas Street, and made up a ballad for the occasion on the spot.

Although blind, he was married twice, gaining a step-daughter and begetting a son, Michael, who went to sea for some years. Zozimus, his wife and step-daughter and son occupied the top back room of No. 17, Patrick Street, where he resided for many years, and ultimately died, on the sixth day of December, 1870.

He acquired his name from the story, popular at the time, *The Extraordinary Life, Conversion, and Death, of the Great Penitent, St Mary of Egypt, who was discovered in the wilderness, in the fifth century, by the pious Zozimus, an ecclesiastic, who devoted his days to solitude and devotion.*

Now, there's a title for you! This account was written in the seventeenth century by the Right Rev. Dr Coyle, Catholic Bishop of Raphoe. It was taken from the *Acta Sanctorum*, Challoner's *Britannia Sancta*, and Butler's *Lives of the Saints*. Zozimus gave his own rendition of this tale in ballad form.

I wandered through the Dublin of Zozimus, imagining the River Poddle as it then was, with its five mouths, and the women washing their clothes on its banks in what is now the Coombe, and the crowds gathering in the evenings to heckle the great balladeer, who was the television of his day. All this wandering was in preparation for *My Name is Zozimus*, which went off at half cock.

It was particularly frustrating, because Joe O'Donnell, the playwright, had written a great script, and I felt that it had been wasted. I asked him if he would write a one-man show for me about Zozimus, and he agreed. I was delighted, because I was obsessed with the character, and indeed still am. It was a huge study, but the imagery in it was so strong that I never lost my way, because I saw it as a series of vivid pictures. Once you could see the pictures, the text just poured out.

Tomás directed and lit the show, now called simply *Zoz*, and he even designed the settings. He was a tower of strength. We worked a long and hard rehearsal schedule, and opened in the Peacock Theatre. But unfortunately we coincided with one of the longest and hottest heat waves of the century, and except for the invited audience on the opening night, virtually nobody came. The show got good notices in all the papers, but you couldn't defeat a heat wave like this one. I certainly wouldn't have gone to see myself, even out of loyalty!

Frank in the Wicklow Mountains
Photograph by Emmet Bergin

Frank, front row right, with his family on
the steps of their home, Rosemount,
Avoca Avenue, Blackrock

Frank, aged 3

Frank's father, Charles E. Kelly (C.E.K.),
sketching for the popular satirical magazine,
Dublin Opinion

Frank, aged 3

Graduating from UCD in 1961 with a Bachelor's
degree in Law

Frank, second from left, on the day of his First Holy
Communion in Sion Hill, Blackrock

The wedding of Frank and Bairbre in Drumcondra, in 1964. With Aideen and Fíona as flower girls, David Kelly as best man and Rosaleen Linehan as bridesmaid

Bairbre and Frank in their twenties

Frank in costume for *Hall's Pictorial Weekly*, striking a pose

In *Hall's Pictorial Weekly*, with Paul Murphy and Eamon Morrissey

With Dermot Morgan, Ardal O'Hanlon and Pauline McLynn during the *Father Ted* days. *Photograph courtesy of Hat Trick Productions*

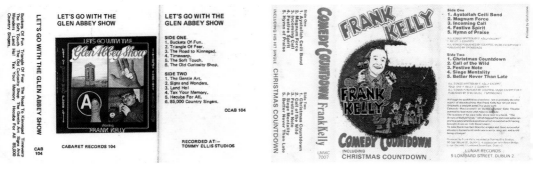

A cassette from Frank's popular radio programme, *The Glen Abbey Show*

A cassette containing 'Christmas Countdown', featuring Frank's famous Gobnait O'Lunacy character

A painting of Frank as Parnell Mooney, the crazed county councillor from *Hall's Pictorial Weekly*

A recent portrait of Frank

Frank and Bairbre with their seventeen grandchildren. From left to right and top to bottom: Stephanie, Holly, Sophie, Jack, Emily, Gillie, Sarah, Leo, Charlie, Max, Amy, Daniel, Felix, Caragh, Harvey, Myles and Zach in Bairbre's arms

I have full confidence that it was a good show, and I am not using the heat wave, solely, for the show's box office failure. We had booked the Opera House to follow the Peacock, and Tomás and I made our arrangements to have the scenery transported to Cork, and headed down there to await its arrival.

Of course it was madness on my part to even dream of the Opera House, because it was such a huge venue to fill for a one-man show, but then inexperience is a great teacher.

On the Sunday morning, Tomás and I went to the Opera House to set up, but there was no sign of the set. It had not arrived from Dublin. I phoned John Slemon, who was in charge of such matters at the Abbey, and it transpired that the movers had arrived at the Peacock with a van which was too small for the purpose, and left without even a message to us.

I was panicking, and asked John Slemon what the hell I was going to do. He said not to worry. He would send it down by Abbey Transport (the name was a coincidence), and this he did. It travelled through the wee hours of the night to Cork, and arrived in the early hours of Monday morning. I will always be indebted to him.

We assembled the set, Tomás put in the lighting plot, and we opened that night to an empty house, during a prodigious heat wave, and that was the way it was for the following week. I have never played to less business, except one time when there was the greatest blizzard of the century, but I have no regrets. I loved the script and I love it still, but you can't get an audience in when you can fry an egg on the pavement outside.

Having been defeated by a heatwave with *Zoz*, I never imagined that anything similar would happen to me again, but this time I was able to share my chagrin with another actor, and of course, the director.

Pat Laffan had asked me to play the role of Frank in Willy Russell's *Educating Rita* at the Gate Theatre, opposite the late Susan Fitzgerald as Rita. I was delighted with the opportunity. There is something very satisfying about getting into the very guts of a play, with just one other actor and the director. It is so much easier to remain focussed when there is a big, sprawling production.

Susan was great to work with, and all was looking good when we opened. Her notices were deservedly much better than mine, because she gave a towering performance. However, we were not long playing when the country was hit by an immense blizzard. All business ceased at the Gate. No one in their right senses would have ventured out, so bad were the icy winds and the snow.

I would collect Susan each evening at her house in Rathgar, and I would drive in second gear all the way to the theatre, where we would wait for an official pronouncement as to whether there would be a performance or not, and then we would head home, because no audience would have shown up, in spite of the good advance bookings. So bad were the weather conditions that there were big mechanical diggers at work, removing the ice in big slabs from O'Connell Street. When the blizzards abated and we resumed playing, Susan discovered that she was pregnant, and her doctor didn't think that it would be advisable for her to continue in the play. She was a huge loss in a two-hander play, and her substitute would have to come in 'on the book', which would be no easy task in a vehicle like *Educating Rita*.

Ruth Hegarty joined us, with tremendous style and endurance. It was an amazing achievement to give a good performance of such a demanding role with the script in her hand, but this she did, to a great audience reaction. She was fully into the part in no time. It is impossible to compare her performance to that of Susan, because they were two entirely different performances by two completely different kinds of actors.

$$—\!\!\!\sim\!\!\!— \quad 25 \quad —\!\!\!\sim\!\!\!—$$

Fraught Comedy

The relationship between actor and director can be a very fraught one, and sometimes the possibility of improving it can be quite outside one's control. Gerry Sinnott asked me to play the role of Stanley Gardener, in what is, in my humble opinion, Ray Cooney's best farce, *Run for Your Wife*. The cast comprised Des Keogh, Ann Sinnott (now Williams), Mary Kearns, Christopher Barritt, Des Nealon, Frank Melia and Patrick Chambers.

Our director was from London, and had directed several productions for Ray Cooney before. On his way in from Dublin, his taxi driver asked him what had brought him to Dublin. The director told him, and he asked who were his cast in the show. When he mentioned my name, the taxi man became ecstatic. He was a fan of mine and had followed *Hall's Pictorial Weekly* (a long-running TV show) and the *Glen Abbey Radio Show* religiously, and had seen me on the stage. He waxed lyrical, telling the director that I was the greatest thing since free love, and bored the face off him all the way into Dublin city talking about me.

Now, what people think, or like, is a matter for themselves, but the director arrived at rehearsals with the fixed impression that I would be 'outside the play', as he put it later. His attitude to me was cautious to say the least.

The show was a huge success. Bairbre used to come in many nights just for the therapy of hearing the laughter. We took it to the

Opera House in Cork, where it played to capacity business, as it had in Dublin.

Time elapsed and I was playing the role of Squire Sullen in *The Beaux' Stratagem* at the Abbey. My tormentor was due back to direct another of Gerry Sinnott's productions, which would open in the Olympia after *The Beaux' Stratagem* had finished. One night there was a knock on the door of my dressing room after the show, and when I opened it, there he stood. He looked at me without any sign of humility, and said: 'I was mistaken. You can act.'

It was such a relief. I had waited all those months for his dictum! What he didn't know about acting is that everybody has the right to be wrong. If you become an actor, you do so at your own risk. You are going to do it regardless of what anyone else thinks. You have the right to succeed or fail. I have never wished the personal rejections which I have experienced in a long acting career on any of my offspring. I didn't encourage them, and I didn't discourage them.

It isn't unlike lending your car to someone. You fear that they will crash, but you are convinced that you won't crash yourself. I have often said, in a lecture which I have been asked to give to young people about the business of being an actor, that no one cares a damn if you resign or not, and if they notice they will soon forget.

It would be a pity to look back on a life with no memories of holidays and happy family occasions. It is time to think of giving it up when it is not delivering any worthwhile quality of life. The length of time you allow yourself to find out is your own business. Acting is not like being a painter. It is a co-operative art form, and many things have to function well for it to succeed. If you want to paint, you can get on with it yourself, but bear in mind that van Gogh didn't sell many paintings in his lifetime.

The Beaux' Stratagem was well staged and acted, but it just didn't do the business. We were all quite crestfallen at the poor attendance, and were in for a rehearsal of some part of it which, it was felt, might be improved. There is a coffee area near the rehearsal room, and we were all gloomily sipping during a break when the Artistic Director at the time came toddling along, holding his coffee mug between his two hands.

He stopped and said: 'Great news everyone!'

We all thought that there had been a sudden upsurge in ticket sales. He smiled shyly, and then said: 'There was a snowdrop in our garden this morning!'

26

America

I have heard it said by musicians that their manager just took some darts and threw them at the map at random, and that this was why they had to play Donegal one night, Cork the next, and then Galway, and so on. This might be said of a tour of the United States which I did with the late and former Abbey actress, Ronnie Masterson, widow of Ray McAnally. We just had to book venues in order of availability.

I have already mentioned 'Matchmaker', Ray's adaptation of the letters of John B. Keane, which I had toured throughout Ireland with Anna Manahan. Ronnie had the option for the rights for the US, and asked me to tour it with her. I was delighted to accept the invitation.

Ronnie was a rock of strength, highly computer-literate and organised, without which virtues the tour would have been impossible. We flew to Kennedy Airport, and were to make our way to the terminal for Chicago. To our shock we discovered that this was so far away that we couldn't possibly hope to make our connection. We were standing in something close to despair, when I made an inquiry of a nearby official, in a really smart uniform, about the availability of transport.

He was a nice guy, polite and helpful. I showed him our schedule, and he shook his head sadly. We hadn't a chance. Then there came divine intervention. He turned to me and scrutinised my face.

'You're not Frank Kelly, are you?'

'Yes I am, but how could you know me?'

'I'm Dermot Watchorn, your friend Emmet Bergin's cousin. We met a couple of times when I was in Dublin.'

'My God, I didn't recognise you in the uniform!'

'Hang on,' he said, taking out a mobile phone and dialling a number. We only had to wait a minute or two before a huge limo slid up. He bundled us and our cases into it, and I only had time to wave goodbye to him through the back window. We made it in time to catch our connection. I could never thank him enough.

We stayed in suburban Chicago, in my first experience of an American house. To me, it seemed like a huge garden gazebo, with a tower in one end of it. I had never seen wooden housing like this before, except on the telly.

The interior was pure Norman Lincoln Rockwell, the furnishings old-fashioned, with antimacassars on the backs of the chairs, an ormolu clock on the mantelpiece, and heavy green drapes on the windows. It had that 1880s look you see in Western movies, and which I was to encounter quite a few times during my travels throughout the United States. Of course, this look came from Europe, with the massive immigration in the second half of the nineteenth century.

Ronnie and I breakfasted in a diner the following morning, where we sat with huge trucks trundling by, their wheels half the height of the windows. The interior was ill-lit and gloomy by Dublin standards. The only thing missing was Humphrey Bogart at the next table, as the waitress minced over to us on stiletto heels, her face made up to make her look quite like Dorothy Lamour.

She handed us the menu and I smiled without opening it. 'Don't tell me,' I said, 'you're not really a waitress? You're an actress, aren't you?'

Had she been able to swell any more with pride she would have burst the buttons on her blouse.

'Hey, how did you guess, sir? Do I really look that much like an actress?'

'Oh,' I said, 'there's a look. You can always tell.'

I began to giggle then, and she asked me if everything was alright. I explained that I would be able tell much of what was on the menu without even opening it, although this was my first breakfast in America.

She asked me to try, and I made a fair effort, with hash browns, pancakes and syrup, eggs over easy, etc.

'How can you guess?' she said.

'I saw it in the movies,' I replied, and it was true. It was literally like being in an old Paramount movie. So great had been our immersion in American movies that there was a constant déjà vu feeling. These films were a really formative influence in our education.

It is interesting to remember that these images were formed when there was a somewhat jaundiced view taken of the film industry by the Church in Ireland. I well remember being asked to write an essay on 'The Evils of the Silver Screen' in school. Perhaps this shows that it is better to try and incorporate the best of what is new in education, rather than to treat it with suspicion. Films are now considered as 'art', and there are many people who would be surprised to think that we were asked to write such an essay.

It was my job to light the show. This was easy when there was a computerised lighting board, but quite difficult at times, when all the cues had to be punched in. It depended on the lighting man (with one exception they were men). When I met a 'dude' with a baseball cap back-to-front on his head, who was really 'cool', and who said things like 'yup' and 'piece of cake', it was time to become really suspicious. It usually meant a long and difficult day.

Actually, the lighting person in Chicago was a woman with boundless energy and goodwill. Doing the 'get-in' to the theatre was difficult because the lighting was somewhat primitive, but this marvellous woman worked miracles, hanging light after light.

The stage settings were simple enough, but being the kind of play it was, it only required a table and three chairs, and a bench, or what we call a 'form'. However, many Americans had little idea of what you would find in a Kerry cottage kitchen of the forties, and we would find that they had gone to great trouble to find a mahogany table and three upholstered chairs. It was often difficult to explain what was required, and particularly to do so without giving offence.

I had cause to go in and out of the auditorium's doors many times while we were hanging the lights, and was constantly molested by a jovial, elderly character, who thought that my name was the funniest thing he had ever heard since his grandmother had caught her tits in the wringer. He would stand in my way every time I went thought the door, laughing heartily and saying: 'Well, I'll be damned. Frank Kelly! Hey, if that don't beat all! That sure is a real "Irish" name. Frank Kelly. Hey, if that don't beat all! Sure, that is a real "Irish" name! Frank Kelly! Well, I'll be damned!'

We would do a side-stepping act and go around each other, and the bile would rise even higher in me every time it occurred. What made it even more infuriating was the fact that he was dressed, believe it or not, in a sparkling white boiler suit, with a bunch of bright green shamrock embroidered on his breast pocket. St Patrick's Day was looming at the time.

Then an evil thought dawned on me. The boiler suit must be his pride and joy. How would he react to a threat to dirty it up for him? I could hear him approach to block my way again, when I ducked back into the theatre, and then, as fortune would have it, found a full ashtray on the table. I scooped the contents into my hand, and stood in the doorway.

'Hey, if it isn't Frank Kelly! Well, that's a real "Irish" name! Well, if that isn't a good one!'

I grinned and said: 'I guess a guy who owns a while boiler suit would be as mad as hell if someone rubbed cigarette ash all over it!'

He stared in horror at the ash in my hand as I approached him, saying: 'Hell, a nice guy like you wouldn't dirty up my suit, would you?'

'Try me,' I said, still grinning manically as I approached him. He turned in panic, breaking into a trot.

'Hey, come on, I was only kidding!'

His pace increased as he heard me breaking into a trot behind him.

'You're crazy, d'ye know that?'

He ran into the street and I continued to pursue him. I followed him all the way to the end of the block, before I turned back. He never reappeared. There is one mature Chicagoan who remains convinced to this day that he was pursued by a mad Irishman.

In the Irish Cultural Centre, Conor Cruise O'Brien was giving a lecture, and as we entered we were harassed by protesters, who told us that we were not to listen to that guy, O'Brien. He was against Irish republicanism and the ould sod. He was pro-British and would sell us out tomorrow.

These were obviously Americans of Irish descent, but when I conversed with them, I realised that, for all they knew about the modern Ireland, they might as well have been talking about Hawaii.

We met Maeve Binchy and her husband, writer Gordon Snell, there, with whom I had written the *Only Slaggin'* radio show for many years, along with Eamon Morrissey and Jim Doherty. We also had the pleasure of meeting our esteemed president of the time, Mary Robinson, with whom we had a very pleasant and amusing conversation, which was interrupted by the committee queen par excellence, who hinted that perhaps we were monopolising the president, and that maybe we would like to mix a little more with the general company.

We stood uncertainly for about one second, until Mary Robinson said that she was talking to her friends from Dublin, and that she would circulate when she was ready. We had been talking for about ten minutes, and ten minutes later I was revelling in the discomfiture of the committee lady, as too, I suspect, were Gordon and Maeve.

Chicago was followed by Albany, where we stayed with a lady named Polly Noonan, of mature years, but indomitable. She was retired and a widow, having served as personal assistant to the mayor for some thirty years. She and her husband had originally owned many acres of land, some of which had been acquired by the city, under compulsory purchase, or what the Americans call 'eminent domain'.

They had retained a good few acres within the city limits, and these had absolute privacy. They were allocated among her offspring who had built beautiful homes on them. It seemed an intelligent thing to do with such a valuable asset.

Polly had a pool on her land, with canoes on it for her grand-children. It was an idyllic place for children to play in, but there was a problem.

There is a macho breed of American, who lives a fantasy life as a great white hunter, and apparently any wooded expanse of land is fair game when the season comes.

Whatever kind of wildlife there was on her land had attracted their attention, and I was astonished when I saw a line of bullet holes in one of the canoes. It wouldn't be unlike owning a big garden in Foxrock and being invaded by mad marksmen in search of blue tits. Apparently the dreams of frontier life live on.

One day I decided to go for a jog around the perimeter of the entire estate. I have always been intrigued by the fact that these lands were occupied by native Americans such a short time ago, by our standards. What is old to Americans seems so much more recent to Europeans.

A case in point was when a friend of mine, who is a singer of renown, was on a coach tour of the US. They stopped somewhere, and the driver said: 'We've got some time to spare, so I guess you guys might like to go around to the back of the block. There's some very interesting nineteenth century houses there.'

My friend looked at him with scorn, saying: 'I've got socks older than that!'

Anyway, my jog took me to what I imagined must have been the original road, before the great highway nearby was constructed. I followed it, and it gave me a great view of all the cars whizzing by. The hard shoulder was littered with the sidewalls of burst tyres. I sat on the border barrier to view them and catch my breath.

Then, being of a curious disposition, I stepped on to the hard shoulder to get a better view of the traffic. I trotted along for a few yards, until I heard an amplified voice saying: 'Stop exactly where you are, and walk directly towards me!'

The humour of this command struck me immediately. How the hell could you stand exactly where you were, and walk towards someone at the same time? I turned to see two enormous state troopers on the central reservation, one of them sporting a loud hailer. They didn't look as though they had much of a sense of humour. There was no chance of sharing a joke with them about standing where you were and walking towards someone at the same time.

I stood looking at them, and there was a further command: 'Keep your hands out from your sides, and walk towards us buddy.'

Now there I was, with my hands held out, in a plastic transparent top and skimpy shorts, confronted by two huge state troopers. I had to walk through the traffic, at some peril, to the central reservation, where I was stuffed into a patrol car.

'You have committed a crime, buddy,' I was told.

'What crime have I committed?' I asked, bewildered, and not a little annoyed at being called 'buddy'. I have an aversion to such familiar terms. It is not unlike being addressed as 'friend' in a Belfast pub. There is nothing so unfriendly. It really means that you are just about to be hit, and very hard. However, there was little enlightenment in the eyes of these two, so I didn't dare to object.

'You have been running too near the highway, buddy, and that's against the law of this country.'

'But I'm a visitor in this country. I didn't know.'

'That is not our concern, buddy. You are in the United States of America now, and you are obliged to obey our laws.'

I realised that these two guys were not alone very stupid, but also very annoyed on behalf of the US of A.

They questioned me for no less than an hour and a half, and then drove me towards my hostess's place.

'Where do we drop you, buddy?'

'Noonan Lane,' I replied.

Then they exchanged glances. The name 'Noonan' obviously meant something to them.

As we pulled up, I asked: 'Where is the handle on the door of this car?'

'Don't you know that there is no handle on the inside of a patrol car, buddy?'

I felt very angry, and not a little foolish, as they unchildlocked me. When I returned to my hostess's house I was asked for descriptions of them. Now, their descriptions would have fitted any two huge state troopers, and no doubt, you will understand that I hadn't thought of asking them their names. Anyway, I said to Polly: 'They're your troopers, and they have their own way of doing their job. It's different back home.'

27

Texas is Really Big

It was time to fly to Dallas, Texas (more random dart throwing at the map of America). Dallas is, of course, famous for one tragic event. Having been the first in the *Irish Independent* to receive the news of President Kennedy's assassination, I really wanted to see the scene of the book depository and the grassy knoll, and of course, like most much anticipated sights, it was an anti-climax. A building is a building, and the grassy knoll is slightly changed in shape, but quite unremarkable.

For what it's worth, I still believe that there was a second gun. Why? Because right from the very beginning of the drama there was mention of a second gun, and it seemed to be airbrushed out as the story developed. It went from being a fact, to a supposition, to a sensational allegation.

My movie script would show a very aggressive CIA back-room gnome, with the sweat rolling off his chiselled face, telling a minion: 'Kill that story of a second gun, or maybe there will be more than your job on the line. By the way, how are Lucy and the kids?'

I had been asked to lecture in Washburn University for a few days while the show was on. It was an enlightening experience for me, if not for the students, because you have to be awake to listen to a lecture, and they were literally asleep before I opened my mouth. At one point, I asked them whether there was any point of

150

continuing, and one or two of them, who were almost awake, shook themselves from their torpor, with: 'Hey man, keep talking. It's really cool!'

I stumbled on uncertainly, and when the lecture ended, I sought out the professor.

'Aw, you don't want to bother yourself about that, Frank. Many of these people are on a back-to-work course, and many of them have problems. You're doing fine!'

I had the sneaking feeling that many of them might do a hell of a lot better without the help of marijuana. There was one exception, who made the lecturing more bearable. This was a handsome young man, who peppered me with questions after the lectures, and showed an unwavering interest. I was encouraged.

The university was unbelievable. It could only have happened in a very wealthy place. Any Irish academic would have given an arm and a leg for facilities like these. They are renowned for their music school, which is of a top-class standard, and they have two theatres, a large one, which would be an adequate national theatre in most European countries, and a 'small' one, which would pass for a large one in many.

There are literally hundreds of remotely controlled lights in the big one, and almost as many in the small one.

We played in the big one, and the audiences were terrific. Texas is a very welcoming place. I used to go jogging around various neighbourhoods, and there would be housewives constantly hosing down their cars in their 'front yards'. (I always feel that the word 'garden' is so much more descriptive.)

These ladies would frequently initiate a conversation with you, which would be most unusual in most American cities, and unheard of nowadays in most Irish cities. They were really friendly, and bade you a warm welcome to Dallas.

While we were in Dallas, eighteen people were machine-gunned to death in a diner in Fort Worth by some maniac. I was horrified by the news, and when I asked people what they thought of the murders, I was met with: 'Aw, that was miles away. Don't worry yourself,' and the topic of conversation was changed quickly. It reminded me of *Watership Down*, with the rabbits talking frantically when one of their number disappeared.

There are certain sights, which shouldn't be missed, in the desert, near Dallas. One is a sculpture, called Los Collinos, which recreates the crossing of a river by some horses. Water has been diverted to make a realistic ford, and the horses are beautifully sculpted. For some reason, although all is man-made, the scene is truly evocative and memorable.

Not far from this, there is a business complex, again surrounded by desert, which has a large canal running through it, with boat transport available for the inhabitants to go from building to building, or alternatively, there is a funicular railway overhead for the same purpose. How all this can pay its way I'll never know.

Before we left we went for a meal at the top of a very tall building, largely made of glass, again out in the desert. The outlook was lovely, and the cuisine quite splendid, but what was most pleasing was the fact that we were served by the young man who had been asking all the questions at my lectures. He greeted us with: 'Hi, I'm your waiter for the evening. Welcome!'

He was as bright and efficient as he was at my lectures, and I have little doubt that we will see him in Hollywood movies one of these days, if he hasn't made it into one or two already. He had all the necessary drive for a Hollywood acting career.

The Texan weather was in the high eighties, and I was strolling around in my bare feet in someone's garden, with a cool drink in my hand, and a fistful of pecan nuts which I had gathered from the ground. We were heading into April, and I was able to smugly describe this scene to Bairbre at home, on the phone. In the words of Dudley Moore: 'It's always nice to think that there's someone worse off than yourself.'

28

Bad Boys and a Public Affair

The contrast between the temperatures in Dallas and St Paul Mississippi, where we played next, was traumatic. They had experienced the highest snowfall in a hundred years, and when I say high, I mean high! So high was it, that they had to cut streets through it to reveal the original ones underneath, and to allow public transport to continue.

People had never seen its like, and I thought of the pioneers who had travelled across America in their covered wagons. It must have been extraordinarily testing. To think that they could have encountered conditions like these!

We played in the Landmark Theatre, where I encountered one, Randy Seidt, a lighting man who did his job with relish and style. There was no 'cool', and no 'yup' or 'piece of cake', just intelligence and pleasant company.

I dined in The St Paul Grill, where Al Capone and his partners and enemies had dined, having given up their ordnance to a corrupt police chief before crossing the county line. I was served by a young man who was a walking library of information about the period, but he was unable to tell me where they had been arraigned when they had tried to cross back again over the county line.

Everyone in St Paul said, like Col. Oliver North, when I asked them: 'I guess I don't recall that,' while staring at a spot somewhere above my right shoulder.

The Landmark Theatre was an interesting old building, and I am by nature a snooper. Because of the efficiency of Mr Seidt, I had some welcome time on my hands. In many previous venues I had spent more time than I wanted setting up the show. I decided to explore the theatre, and having wandered all over the upstairs part, I descended into its bowels.

I switched on the lighting in an underground corridor, and saw, covered in thick dust, what looked like photographs along the wall. I found some tissues in my pocket, and having dusted off the surfaces as best I could, was astonished to find that they were of Mr Capone and his associates, grinning from ear to ear, in the company of their 'mouthpieces' as they were being led away from the courthouse, quite sure that they would soon be free. Mr Capone, at least, was to die in prison, where he was sent for tax evasion.

Sadly, I don't think that this sort of thing brings closure for society in general. He was known to have been a prodigious murderer, and the police never got him for this. I feel that, where justice is not seen to be done, society is irreparably damaged. A close look at our own society, where known murderers are serving long prison sentences other than for their killings, would seem to indicate that their apparent immunity acts as an inducement to their apprentices to commit more murders, and society seems to lose faith in the ability of the powers of law enforcement to do their job successfully.

On inquiring, I found that the Landmark Theatre had formerly been a courthouse, and that it was here that Capone and friends had been arraigned. I was very excited about this, but it aroused little interest in the people I spoke to about it afterwards. Apparently organised crime, even as historical as this, is not considered a fit subject for after-dinner conversation.

In St Paul, I was the guest of a prominent psychiatrist and his wife, who had a beautiful home on a broad street. It was a brick house, like most of the houses in the area, and it was especially spacious inside, spacious enough to accommodate two Irish wolfhounds, one of which used to put its head in my lap in the evenings. It was a lovely creature, as was its comrade, and I felt honoured by its trust. However, the other dog just didn't like me, for some reason or other. It may have been a jealousy thing. I will just never know. But when a wolfhound growls at you, it is a warning that you take seriously.

My hostess asked me whether I had a problem with dogs, and I assured her that I hadn't. We had an enormous dog at home at the time, called Max, which we fondly remember. He was a cross between a Labrador, and as far as I could guess, a donkey. In his prime, he weighed twelve and a half stone, and stood six feet tall on his hind legs. He looked very intimidating, but in his entire life, he never snapped at anyone; in fact I think that he thought he was human.

One morning we went around to what our hostess called 'the back lane' (in Ireland it would have ranked as a wide street) to get out the car. The street was cordoned off, and we were accosted by a Nicholas Cage double, who told us that we would have to identify ourselves and then be accompanied to our car. He was accompanied by a Bruce Willis double, and it was bulgingly obvious that they were both 'carrying heat'.

It transpired that a US senator was 'visiting with' a glamorous black lady professor in a house further up the street, and these were FBI men who were providing security. They were not the only FBI men. The place was littered with them, all looking exactly like Bruce Willis or Nicholas Cage. It would appear that you can't get into the FBI unless you are impossibly good-looking.

The whole neighbourhood was intrigued by this liaison, especially as the senator was a household name. We had it on good authority that there was a passionate affair taking place. They were still there when we departed from St Paul a few days later. We were amazed that so many men could be detailed to keep watch over one senator's love life, but then America is a big country, and I suppose it's a question of scale.

Later, when I was in Washington, I was seated watching the television with a very wise and experienced lady who had had a long and successful career with the government, reaching a high level before retiring, when there appeared on the screen an item on Judge Thomas, who was being examined as to his moral suitability for a post as a Supreme Court judge.

Thomas was a black man, and there was an allegation that he had made improper advances towards a young lady some years before being proposed for the Supreme Court position.

There was a kind of moral jury, evaluating his character, and there, right in the middle, was the senator who had been 'visiting with' the black lady, while we had been in St Paul. Hypocrisy can be brought to a fine art.

We had the honour of playing in the theatre in the World Bank Centre in Washington. Now, the interesting thing about the World Bank Centre is that there is no money there whatsoever, just highly valuable people, who would command huge ransoms. Hence, there is unprecedented security. Each time I went out to the street to get something for the show, I had to face exhaustive questioning on my return, by a gentleman to whom I had been speaking just ten minutes beforehand.

Once I was on the inside of the partition again, he would change personality completely.

'So, how's the show goin' Frank? Is there anything I can do to help? If there is, just you let me know.'

Then I would have to go outside again, and when I returned, the same interrogation would take place without a flicker of recognition on the man's face, and once I was inside we would be friends again. This would seem to be ridiculous, but of course this is the only way to have proper security, and as I have said, there would have been some very good targets for kidnappers there.

Most of the black government employees were truly elegant, of big stature, both men and women. At lunch hour, many of the workers would go to a gym, where they gave intimidating exhibitions of fitness. Having trained in gyms all my life, I felt very inferior indeed to these specimens.

When the curtain went up, the entire audience was composed of black people, and they hung on every word of John B. Keane's text, laughing aloud and giving rapturous applause at the final curtain. You wouldn't have got a finer reception in Kerry!

I had carried a bottle of J&B scotch whiskey through many states, but had never had the chance to open it. America is not really a great drinking country. In many homes I was asked whether I would like a bourbon by the man of the house, only to see his wife's knuckles whiten. I would say: 'Only if you are having one yourself,' to which the reply would be: 'Well, I guess I might have one of you are having one.'

When I got this answer I would invariably reply: 'I guess I'll just have a cream soda.' There would be an audible sigh of relief from the wife, and smiles of approval. She would have been reassured that I was not 'an enabler'. It would appear that there are a great many men in their early fifties in America who have lost one empire through drink, and who are on their second chance. Also, there is a tradition of puritanism in many states, which dies hard on the drink issue. But there is always the exception, thank the good God!

One night I was seated with my Washington hostess when she asked would I like a drink of whiskey. I was delighted to accept, but even more pleased when it transpired that it was J&B. There was a little less than a third of a bottle, and we finished it.

With some hesitation I asked her: 'Would you care for another drink? I have a litre of that whiskey in my case upstairs, if you wouldn't feel that it was a criticism of your hospitality.'

Her face assumed a business-like expression as she said: 'Get it.' I was delighted, as it had been a pretty dry trip so far. We made a fair impression on that bottle of whiskey. This lady had risen to the top, working for the government, and could hold her own with the men of her time, and her liquor like a trooper. We swapped anecdotes and jokes until the small hours, and it was a pleasant change from the politeness which I had encountered since arriving in America.

Just before I left Washington, I phoned the Gaiety Theatre in Dublin to reply to an invitation from a lovely lady, named Aileen Connors, to appear in the pantomime, *Jack and the Beanstalk*, with Twink. I explained to the girl at the other end that I was phoning from Washington, but she told me that Aileen was in another room, nearby, and that I would have to call back.

I repeated, with an edge to my voice, that I was calling from Washington, and asked her to go into the other room and say to Aileen that I was on the phone. She did as bidden, and Aileen and I concluded a deal.

They do business differently in the USA.

29

Big People and a Scary Garage Door

Having been reared with *The Saturday Evening Post* magazine and the illustrations of Norman Lincoln Rockwell, I was eager to see the American agricultural community up close, and I got my chance when we went to Topeka, Kansas. This is really out in the prairie: more covered wagon country, in my imagination. In fact, it is really cereal crop country. There are huge grain silos against the skyline everywhere, and sweetcorn growing right up to the roadside. The Kansas farming people are real, wholesome, 'country folk'. Of course, in Topeka itself there were smaller and slicker city dudes, but that's the city.

Having travelled around the States, I gathered the impression that a big environment breeds bigger people. The country people fascinated me. Both the men and the women were big-boned and handsome. I was in a few farmers' houses, and their wives actually wore aprons with floral patterns on them and smelled of fresh baking.

In one home, I sat opposite a truly huge man. He was carrying no spare fat, and looked really fit. I felt like a Lilliputian in the presence of Gulliver. His hands were of a formidable size, with huge, perfectly-formed fingernails. His teeth had big divisions between them, his eyes were Nordic blue, and he had a great head of grey curly locks. In fact, he was straight off the cover of *The Saturday Evening Post*. I remember trying not to lose the thread of the conversation as I thought: 'I never knew they made jeans that size!' There was enough material in them to make a tent for a small family. His wife was to scale, blonde, blue-eyed and beautifully proportioned.

She was obviously of Scandinavian origin. These people remind me of a book by Ole Edvart Rolvaag, entitled *Giants in the Earth*, in which he describes the Norwegian settlers moving west, and how, because the prairies were an ocean of grass, they navigated by the stars.

There was no acoustic in this giant ocean of grassy hillocks, and little children who wandered too far from their wagons were never seen again, because they couldn't hear their families calling for them. Eventually they evolved the practice of paying out a reel of cotton when they attended to a call of nature, so that they could find their way back.

I love land, and when I told some friends this, the farmer said: 'Ye like land? Hell, how long are you stayin'? We can get in my plane and I'll take ye out to see some of my sections' (their term for land holdings). I would have loved this, but unfortunately it was too near the end of our stay. Maybe I'll get back there some day.

Of course, side by side with this rustic idyll was accommodation for the city folk, who worked in offices. They consisted of huge suburban housing developments, one of them, in which I stayed, built in a circle out in the prairie, and all backing on to an artificially created lake. Each house had a jetty at the end of the backyard, to which was moored a thirty- to forty-foot gin palace, and on the summer nights – or 'white nights' – when there is virtually no darkness, they stay out on these boats drinking all night.

My hosts were wonderfully hospitable and hard-working. They worked in the city, and left early in the morning. There is such white light out there that the houses are left in stygian gloom while their occupants are away during the day, with the blinds pulled and the air conditioning full on. I was leaving later in the morning, so I had to put in a little time before I left for the city.

When I was departing, I had to bring outfits for about three identities. There were casual clothes for the day, work clothes for the get-in, and a lighting plot, and then more formal clothes for the reception after the show. I had to remember to bring felt pens, a biro and notebook, and God knows what else.

Now, the difficulty was that these people had a garage of commercial proportions. It would have held six to eight cars. The door was operated by a small switch at the top of a small stairs at the back of the garage, which led to the kitchen. The idea was to hit the switch, run down the now empty garage and chuck a load under the door, before it landed on my head. It was different for the owners, who were able to merely zap the door from their cars.

I had to line up my piles of belongings at the door, and then head back to the switch. It was imperative that I have everything I needed ready, because there was no going back once the door began to descend, and I had no house key.

The piles of clothes were all in position, and I trotted back to the switch, which I activated. I ran to the door, chucked out my clothes, and then remembered with horror that my wallet was on the kitchen counter. I had no option but to go back for it. The door was descending slowly, as I sprinted back and got it.

It had just never dawned on me to reactivate the door, and like a fool I just ran for the rapidly narrowing gap. I just made it out in a parachute roll. There was no one around, and if I had succeeded in getting a leg pinned under the door, I would have been there until late evening when my hosts would return from work. These are lonely moments, when grown men whimper for their mammies, unheard.

I encountered a wonderful woman in Topeka, who exemplified the American way of life, or at least one aspect of it. She was a retired anaesthetist of sixty-five or seventy years, and her husband was still working as a consultant in a nearby hospital. 'To provide for her old age,' as she put it, she had acquired the franchise for a chain of pizza huts, spread over a vast area.

We had lunch with her, and then she looked at her watch outside the restaurant, saying: 'Well, duty calls. Pizza huts don't run themselves,' and jumped into her car, driving down a dusty road and over the horizon. I couldn't imagine a retired anaesthetist living like that in Ireland. It is easy to say that there is more to life than money, but she was very much alive. Maybe it was that she was having fun earning it.

30

Achill Island and Niagara Falls

Cleveland proved itself to be a great contrast to Topeka, with its overview of Lake Eyrie. The Irish people in Cleveland are largely descended from people who emigrated there from Achill Island in Ireland. True, there are others of different county descent, but the majority would seem to be Achillians.

I met some sad exiles in Cleveland. They found it hard to afford the cost of living, not being highly paid in America, and rarely got home. When they arrived at Shannon, they found the cost of living prohibitive. There was something sad and lonely about them.

I expressed a desire to hear Mass on Sunday when I was in Cleveland, and was told to catch the 11 a.m. one. It was Fr O'Rooney's Mass (not his real name), and was 'mighty fun altogether'. What, I asked, could be so different about Fr O'Rooney's Mass, and was told: 'Oh, you'll see. He's a great guy!'

I could happily have fire-hosed Fr O'Rooney off the altar. He had a fund of the most trite wise-cracks, and could have bored God to death if he had put his mind to it. I found myself looking at a one-man version of *The All Priests Show*, but, remember, this was all done while he was saying Mass. The consecration seemed to be a boring detail which had to be got through before he continued to display his comedic talents.

I have to say that I find Mass a much more spiritual experience when no one is trying to make it 'more interesting'. You may add

163

a little ceremonial liturgy, but not too much for me, thank you. I suppose it is a matter of taste. The original breaking of bread and drinking of wine couldn't have taken too long, so perhaps there is a measure of self-indulgence in overly prolonging it. One thing is sure: it hardly requires the addition of bad music hall gags.

I fled from the car park afterwards in case I would re-encounter Fr O'Rooney's fan club. I am happy to say that these shenanigans would not go down too well in modern Ireland.

A kind friend brought us down to see Lake Erie up close, and it was most impressive. Mind you, the signs that your swim might result in death by pollution made me feel uncomfortable, and I was mesmerised by the sight of anglers catching large silver fish, and promptly throwing then back in again.

We were approached by a guy on a bicycle, who asked us whether we wanted to buy some nice watches and jewellery. Our American friend, who was reassuringly streetwise, asked where the watches and jewellery were, and our cyclist friend opened his coat to reveal an El Dorado pinned to its lining.

The suggestion by my friend that perhaps the cops might be interested in buying some of them as well had a galvanising effect. I had never seen wheel-spin from a bike before.

I had always wanted to see Niagara Falls, and it was well within driving distance from Cleveland, but with the timescale allowed by our schedule, it was unlikely that we would get to see this amazing sight. The more we thought about it, the more our determination grew to see it. Our hosts, the Irish American Cultural Society, had planned a 'brunch' at a lovely country club, but were uncertain as to what time it might end.

If we could merely make it a 'lunch', it would end much earlier. While I couldn't quite get my head around this concept, I pressed for a 'lunch', and with some reluctance they agreed. I got the impression that the 'brunch' would have taken all day, and that would have precluded any chance of getting to Niagara.

So, we made arrangements with a couple who had a small baby, and access to an old Dodge car, to make the journey. The agreement was that I should buy the gas for this old guzzler, but by our standards the cost was very low. It was well worth the trip.

One of the things that struck me again, as we drove up the highway, was that there are so many beat-up cars in America. I never saw so many as on that trip. I even saw one car, completely overloaded with Hispanics, which actually had a wing missing, and it was a bizarre sight to see this leviathan of the highway with one wheel visible as it sailed past the state troopers. You wouldn't get five hundred yards down the M50 in Ireland in it, without the Gardaí pulling you over.

When we reached Niagara I was in my element. I had always wanted to wear the standard issue yellow raincoat and stand behind the waterfall, looking out through the water, just like Marilyn Monroe and George Cotton in the movie *Niagara*, singing 'Kiss, kiss me, say you'll miss, miss me …' The experience was great, but the tourists around me were looking distinctly uneasy, and my companion, Ronnie Masterson, had quietly distanced herself from me. You couldn't have blamed her!

$-w-$ **31** $-w-$

A Cold Frontier Land

After Cleveland, our destination was St John's, Newfoundland. We flew out through Toronto. It brought back memories of my first visit there, when I had performed a one-man show, specially compiled for the occasion of St Patrick's Day.

I found it to be the most democratic place in the world. There was a group playing traditional music in Eirinn's Pub in St John's, comprising an anaesthetist on the bodhrán, a street sweeper on the local percussion instrument, called 'The Dirty Stick', a carpenter on some other instrument, and so on. These guys were close friends, and played there every week. There is a college of music in St John's which produces fine classical musicians, and in their spare time they play in the pubs, particularly in Eirinn's. The standard of musicianship is tremendously high. The violin players can all play the instrument in all the positions, and you will hear wonderful renditions of old, slow Irish airs.

Sometimes there will be a slight difference in the melody, and you will say to yourself: 'No, there's something wrong there. That's a mistake,' and then it will dawn on you that the tune was brought there by someone from Youghal, or Waterford, in Ireland, as far back as the early eighteenth century, and this may be the correct version, having changed since in Ireland.

I was taken out to see Conception Bay, and Flatrock, where Pope John Paul II blessed the fishing fleet, and out to the eastern-most point of the entire continent of America. It was deep into wintertime on my first visit, and I encountered a unique frontier ethic. Every time we stopped and got out to look at the view, two or three cars would pull in to see whether we had broken down. You always check there, in the winter. The next time it could be you, and people need each other.

I expressed a desire to do a small trek on my own, and was provided with a thermal suit and boots. I set off down a narrow gorge, down which ran a river, towards a place called Quidi Vidi, on the ocean. The gorge was hung with stalactites on either side, with the temperature twenty degrees below. I had my mouth covered to prevent the choking feeling which comes when your breath freezes on the way to your lungs. The trip proved to be very rewarding when I reached the little fishing port at the river's end.

At the mouth of the harbour, there is a constantly standing wall of water where the river's flow meets the ocean. This varies from about six to ten feet in height, depending on the tide, the local fishermen power up their boats and punch their way out through it to the ocean to ply their perilous trade. I would sooner them than me!

While I had the thermal suit, I decided to climb Signal Hill, to the station where Marconi's first radio signal across the Atlantic from Ireland was received. Conditions were terrible. There was a blizzard blowing, and forecasts of more, but I was undeterred, being within the confines of the city, and not out in the wilds.

At times the winds were so strong that I had to literally cling to the ground, but I made it to the top. Now, I don't want to make myself sound heroic, because the hill is not much higher than Killiney Hill, in Dublin, but there is no cover on the way up, and a Newfoundland blizzard has to be experienced to be believed. I arrived at the top, a poor imitation of Sir Edmund Hilary, and made an easier descent.

When I was back for a second visit with Ronnie, we were in a pub called The Ship Inn, when I got into conversation with a local. He asked whether I had been in St John's before. When I told him that I had, when I had been doing a show, he squinted up his eyes, and said: 'Hell, I remember you! You're the crazy bastard that climbed that hill in that blizzard!'

The frontier courtesy in St John's is remarkable. One night I was walking down from the university, which is at the top of a hill above the town. I wanted to meet some friends in The Ship Inn. Now, it isn't hard to find your way around in St John's. The streets are mainly parallel to each other, down the side of a hill, but I just wanted to save myself the trouble of a detour in the extreme cold. I asked directions from what looked like a real backwoods man.

He was very big, with a fur hat, and earmuffs. He offered to accompany me, but I declined, saying that all I wanted was to make sure that I was going in the right direction, but he insisted on accompanying me. We didn't have any conversation on the way, because I could think of nothing to say, and when we arrived at the door, he bowed courteously to me, saying: 'In Newfoundland, we like to take care of our visitors, sir.' He had come quite some distance out of his way.

As it was explained to me by an emigrant doctor friend, there is very little serious crime there, because there is literally nowhere to run to. If you robbed a bank in St John's, you would have to have a state-of-the-art chopper standing by, and then you would have to refuel before crossing the Gulf of St Lawrence.

Most of the crime is petty, and when it occurs nearly everybody knows, locally, who did it. There is, however, constant patrolling of the desolate islands off the coastline, which are used as staging posts by drug traffickers, trying to bring their cargoes into the US. The scoring rate of the Canadian Coastguard is very high, but in spite of their efforts there is a fairly steady flow into America.

I only experienced one setback in human relations in Newfoundland, and that was in my entry through the airport at St John's, on my first visit. I was to do a one-man show there, and when I was asked the purpose of my visit, my interrogator, who was a French-Canadian of forbidding mien, narrow-faced, with lank hair and slanty eyes, and quite humourless.

I told him that I was doing a one-man show in St John's and he asked me whether or not I was being paid any money. It has always been my policy not to lie to immigration, and I told him that I was receiving a small subsistence cheque.

This information triggered a paranoid suspicion that I was going to work in Canada without a permit, and I was left for long periods behind bars, while there were consultations elsewhere about what they should do with me. He would revisit me again and again, and ask the same set of questions. Throughout this period an individual would stroll past in the distance at frequent intervals, as I looked appealingly at him from behind the bars of my cell, but to no avail.

Eventually my interrogator returned, and I said to him: 'The money I am receiving is purely an honorarium, sir.'

He was all attention. 'A what, sir?'

'An honorarium,' I replied.

'Could you write that down for me, sir?'

'Certainly, sir' (churlish to refuse!).

And I did. He took the piece of paper away with him for a seemingly endless wait, and then returned. He shook my hand, saying: 'Thank you, sir. I wish to thank you for giving us a precedent.' Now, I have met bureaucrats in my life, but he beat all of them.

I asked him what would have happened to me if I had been unable to give him a precedent, and he replied: 'I guess I would have put you on an aircraft for home.'

When I entered the main reception hall at the airport to meet my hosts, it transpired that they had been given absolutely no information as to my whereabouts during the four-hour period of my detention, and would have been given none had I been deported.

On entering Eirinn's pub one day, the barman said to me: 'May I ask if you are a Mr Kelly?' When I told him that I was, he said: 'What a pity, you have just missed your friend who works at the airport. He's Irish, and he wanted to apologise to you. He wanted to tell you that there was nothing he could have done to help you. He left a pint of Guinness for you as a present.'

It transpired that my benefactor was the individual who had kept walking past at the airport. He had travelled all the way down from the airport to buy me a pint. All I can say to him is: 'Thank you, and if ever I get back I'll buy one for you!'

The summers are short in Newfoundland, but they are consistently fine. Those who make some money all own what they call 'cabins' in the wilderness, and these are beside what they call 'ponds'. We would call them lakes. The wilderness really is a wilderness, because Newfoundland is three times the size of Ireland, and the population is one third the size of Ireland's.

Anyone of a mind to go hunting can buy a rifle, but the regulations are very strict. You may shoot one moose and one caribou in season, but that is the absolute limit. If the police can establish that you didn't fire the shot yourself, then you may expect a heavy fine, confiscation of your rifle, and then your holiday home.

You may cut as much timber as you like for winter fuel, and in what are know as 'the outports', you will see little cabins with timber neatly stacked outside, and pelts hanging up to dry. They look lovely against an indigo blue sky.

These 'outports' are so-called because, before the Canadian highway was built around Newfoundland, these ports were only reachable by ship. The hospital ship would voyage around the entire island, and the surgical cases were taken out to it by boat.

There was a fully equipped operating theatre on board. It all seems rather primitive nowadays, but at least the medical service was brought to the people living in the remote areas. Nowadays it is quite impressive to look at the marker for 'mile one' of the Canadian highway, and to imagine that things were so primitive as late as the Fifties. Many of the medical personnel were Irish, and indeed they still are.

It is commonly known that many of the people in Newfoundland have Irish accents. This is mainly because many of these people travelled there around 1860 or so for the fishing, and stayed. Thus, you will hear an accent not unlike the current Youghal accent there, coming from people who have never been to Ireland, and who have no ambition to go there.

I even heard a Dún Laoghaire accent, yes a Dún Laoghaire accent! There is such a thing. It thickens as you go towards Bray, into something more like a Wicklow accent, but it is really a Dublin accent with certain Wicklow vowels. I met a man named Paddy, with this accent, who had never been to Ireland, and didn't aspire to come here. We were talking one day, and the name 'Cape Basque' was mentioned. Somehow it sounded romantic to me. It is right at the south end of the island, and he had worked there.

I asked him what it was like, saying that the name had an exotic ring to it.

He looked at me with some intensity, and said: 'D'ye know what it's like, Frank?'

I said that I had no way of knowing. Then he said: 'It's the arsehole of the world!' Eat your heart out E. Annie Proulx!

32

Drive-by Shock and 'Kiss and Ride'

I was back in Boston after Newfoundland. Boston was just seething with Irish faces, some of them familiar, and many of them illegally in the US at that time. Fortunately, most, if not all, of them have got their papers by now. Some friends of mine had done really well in business, and had a good standard of living, but couldn't get home to see their ageing parents and other family members.

One night, one of them was telling me about his situation, when he became quite tearful. Many Bostonians would have been astonished to see the soft side of this hard-nosed businessman. Shortly after I returned from America, I was thrilled to hear that he had got his work visa, as had his brother, and they had applied for American citizenship.

Our friends held a garden party for us after the show one night, and it was most pleasant, wandering around with a drink in your hand, with food laid out on trestle tables. Not being a drinker of anything stronger than water or tea, Ronnie went home eventually, but I stayed on, because the craic was mighty and the drink was flowing, most of the crowd being Irish.

Many young people descended on me, wanting to know things about home, and asking me did I know this or that person in Howth, Rathmines or Dublin city. It brought it home to me that Ireland is little more than a townland in comparison to many US states. Towards the end of the evening, I said that I would like to order a taxi, but someone persuaded me to stay a little longer. I was surprised that my company should merit this entreaty, but I gave in and stayed. Eventually I said that I would just have to leave the house, and various muttered phone calls were made, with nods in my direction. Then a taxi was summoned, and I was allowed to depart.

The following day I discovered the reason for my delayed departure. A late arrival at the party had come with some disturbing news. A whole family and their friends had been machine-gunned to death from a limo at the end of the same street while they were barbecuing in the garden. The crime was part of a territorial drugs gang war. I was very glad that I hadn't known the previous night, and I suddenly felt a long way from home.

After this it was Newark, where we encountered a man who told us that he had just acquired a home with an equestrian centre attached. We were invited to a party there, and when we arrived in the early evening, the last rolls of sod were being rolled out for the horses. The house, which was brand-new, was like something from *Gone With The Wind*. There were vast marble staircases at either side of the huge hallway, with mirrors which ran up the whole height of the walls alongside, and a chandelier which would have made Louis Quinze very jealous indeed.

At first I was tempted to sneer, but then why shouldn't this man have his house built this way? He could well afford it, and after all, the great mansions of the Deep South were built quite quickly. More luck to him. In America, all things are possible.

After Newark, Ronnie and I parted, never having exchanged a cross word during the entire odyssey. She flew out to Hollywood to stay with her friend, film actress Jean Simmons, and I stayed with a friend of mine, called Ed Ginty, who works in finance in New York. He lives in Shorthills, which is very posh indeed, and is reached by what is known as the Pathway Train, which connects with the main system at Hoboken, New Jersey.

I travelled into New York to meet up with some of the cast of Brian Friel's *Dancing At Lughnasa*, and spent some pleasant hours with them. It was nice to sit down with Rosaleen Linehan, whose husband, Fergus, was also staying in New York, and Dearbhla Molloy, as well as Gerry McSorley. Fergus and I wandered around New York, watching the skaters in the Rockerfeller Plaza, and doing all the usual tourist things. We encountered one strange sight on our travels.

Strolling along, we came across a record shop, where literally hundreds of my comedy cassettes were displayed in the window, with my ugly mugshot on each of them. I went in and asked the man behind the counter who the distributor was. This was my material, and they were counterfeit covers.

He looked at me with cautious, hooded eyes, and sad: 'Get your ass out of here, buddy, or I'll call the cops.' Realising that I would achieve little by staying, I departed, saying that he would hear from my lawyer. I have never received a dime in royalties for my CDs, vinyl albums, or cassettes from the US, nor have I the means at my disposal to engage the services of an international copyright lawyer, so I will probably never know who was stealing from me.

I had made some purchases to bring home with me, and these were dumped in the Linehans' apartment, which looked out, at a great height, on the Chrysler building. When I had collected my purchases, I took a taxi for Macy's store, under which the train which takes you out to Hoboken, and the Pathway Train, originates. We were almost there when the driver stopped his cab.

'Now sir, here's your train station.' We had stopped in an ill-lit and intimidating slum, outside the most depressingly run-down subway station you could imagine. I explained that I wanted to go to the train station under Macy's. His reply was: 'You want a train station, I give you a train station, mister.'

Now there was no possibility that I would survive unmolested for more than five minutes, encumbered as I was by my purchases, in that hellhole. I refused to leave the taxi unless he dropped me at the required destination, and there followed a row which I will always remember. He threatened to get the cops. He was from the Indian sub-continent, and I told him that half my family was Irish, and the other half was Italian, and that most of them worked in the police force.

Eventually he yielded, and dropped me at Macy's with ill grace. I literally threw the fare at him, and piled out of the taxi. The station in Macy's was little better than the subway station, but I got out to Hoboken, where I wandered about in the dark, looking for the Pathway train station.

I went into a dingy pub, where I encountered the only piece of gratuitous malevolence in my whole odyssey. I asked the proprietor, who had a face like a lizard's, if he would oblige me by telling where the station was. He looked at me for a moment, and then said, quite slowly and deliberately: 'I know where it is, buddy, but I ain't goin' to tell ye.' I couldn't believe my ears, and repeated my inquiry, and was met with: 'For the last time, buddy, I know where it is, but I ain't goin' to tell ye.'

As I was staggering out, totally bewildered, I was accosted by an Irish barmaid, who said: 'I just heard that, mister, and I think it is disgraceful. I'll show you were the Pathway train is.' I cautioned her that perhaps she might lose her job if he knew that she was helping me, but she said: 'The hell with him, mister,' and took me outside, giving me directions. It transpired that the station was directly behind the pub.

As I sat into the carriage, I reflected on my experiences, and thought: 'What a waste of adrenaline that row with the taxi driver was. I could have used all that energy productively, writing, or trying to learn a part. Somehow I don't think I would have the necessary reserves of noradrenaline for life in New York City. It was a relief to return to the sanctuary of Ed Ginty's lovely house.

Now, America, being the land of opportunity, there are many people who mean well but are bluffing when it comes to efficiency in their jobs, and in a way, who can blame them? Who is going to avoid the temptation to 'sex up' their CV, when the facts are true, but can be enhanced by presentation.

Ed had arranged, with characteristic generosity, for a limousine to take me to the airport. He had said that it wasn't worth all the trouble of getting a taxi on my own, and finding the correct terminal under my own steam at Kennedy. The driver duly arrived, wearing white gloves, no less. He was in a highly nervous state, and asked if he could use the telephone.

There followed a prolonged call, while we waited in the hallway. When he reappeared, he greeted me with: 'Hi, I'm your personal chauffeur today.' This came as no surprise to any of us as we loaded my luggage into the trunk of his car. Now, Ed had told me that the fare was on his account, as a gift, for which I was truly grateful, as I had very little cash left. So, we set off for Kennedy.

My chauffeur said to me: 'This is an exciting day for me. It's my first day on the job!' My heart sank. The terms 'cool', and 'piece of cake' sprang to mind. One thing was sure: I knew that I was dealing with total inefficiency from here on in. As we came to the airport, he said to me: 'I guess you will be able to direct me to the right gate, sir. I'm not too familiar with the airport myself.'

I replied coldly: 'No, I will not be able to direct you. That is your job. I am not the chauffeur.' Just then I saw a huge shamrock painted on the side of a building in the distance.

'Make for that shamrock, just make for that shamrock!' I shouted at him. This panicked him and he shouted: 'But what if I miss the turn-off for the shamrock?'

'Just don't miss,' I replied tersely.

He didn't miss it, thanks be to God. When we arrived at the Aer Lingus gate there was sign which read: 'Kiss and ride' (I think such a sign might cause confusion in Ireland.) When we pulled up, he turned to me proffering an invoice book, saying: 'This is not a pre-paid ride, sir,' and told me the fare.

I explained that it was on Mr Ginty's account, and that it certainly was a pre-paid ride.

'I have no knowledge of this, sir.'

Time was ticking by for my check-in, and I was becoming increasingly anxious.

'Just a minute, sir,' he said, 'I will call head office,' and he produced a mobile phone and dialled a number. Then he turned to me and said: 'I guess there is no cover here, sir, so maybe you will pay me, and then you can settle with Mr Ginty later.'

By this time the cops were calling repeatedly on a bull horn: 'Get that fucking automobile away from that stop, or you will be prosecuted!'

I just flipped. 'Open the fucking trunk and I'll get the luggage. I am not going to miss my fucking plane for you.'

The pressure was just too much for him, with the cops shouting that they were going to prosecute him, and he yielded, opening the trunk from the interior, leaving me just enough time to run to the rear of the car and grab my cases, but he accelerated away with my heavy folder, containing the lighting plot of the show, still in the trunk.

I had to abandon the cases on the sidewalk and sprint off after the limo, hammering on the roof to catch the attention of the terrified driver. He opened the window, while the cops kept roaring, and I got him to pull the trunk switch again, and I succeeded in retrieving my lighting plot.

I was flying back business class, and I cannot tell you what it meant to have the use of the Gold Circle lounge to recover from my ordeal. My clothes were soaked with sweat, and I was able to retire for a good under-arm wash, and then have a cool drink before we were called for our flight. I said prayers of thanks to Aer Lingus. 'No frills' my arse! All the frills you have please!

33

Pantomime

Business class was paradise, with drinks served before takeoff, and little socks to wear. (I take a childish delight in these little luxuries.) I was toddling back to my seat from the bathroom, when I encountered a stressed-out Des Keogh. He had been on an extensive tour with his brother-in-law, the late Frank Patterson, tenor, and his wife, Eily O'Grady. I had encountered their promotional literature on my travels.

Jack and the Beanstalk, at the Gaiety Theatre, was a pleasant change from the constant travel, although the baron was not a challenging part. Twink was excellent, of course, but unless you have something to do in it, pantomime can be wearisome.

I have played dame (a comic middle-aged female character in pantomime) in the Olympia, in *Aladdin*, and that was great fun, but that was traditional pantomime, where the Widow Twankey can be as outrageous as she likes. In traditional pantomime, the style is very free, allowing for much improvisation by the dame, and catering for adult audiences as well as children.

In *Cinderella*, I played one of the ugly sisters, opposite Des Keogh, also in the Olympia, and the show was a huge success. We had a lovely, diminutive Cinders in Julie Blunden, who we were able to bully outrageously, to the accompaniment of loud booing from the audience. In the traditional *Cinderella*, the 'uglies' are really a joint dame, and Des Keogh and I certainly got our laughs.

Prior to these shows I was 'feed' to Jack Cruise, as previously stated, and we toured our pantos to Cork, Waterford and Limerick. These shows gave me a chance to write sketches for the stage, instead of radio and TV. It was good experience.

Pantomime really dates from the Middle Ages, when it was performed by 'jongleurs' and mime artists, and the hero was given a magic wand, or 'slapstick', which gave its name to knockabout music hall comedy. The wand was slapped on the stage to give the signal for elaborate scenery changes, which are still a feature of pantomime today.

During the past fifteen years or so, there has been a huge change in pantomime. It is aimed, almost exclusively, at children under the age of about ten, and consists of music geared to the age group, with elaborate dance routines of the pop video idiom, and certainly not the former ballet offerings of the music hall era, or the lines of dancing girls, which followed.

There is no longer a 'political' section for the adults, with tilts at public figures and current affairs, and there is no longer the featured singer, during whose songs all the children went to the lavatory. Hence, in the trade, this repertoire became known as 'the wee-wee songs'.

The modern form certainly works. I played King Jack in *Sleeping Beauty* in 2002, and we did capacity business. The show opened at the beginning of December and finished on February 3, and there was never an empty seat. We did two shows a day, and sometimes three.

Rehearsals were hectic for me, because I had stipulated in my contract that I must be free to fulfil a couple of prior commitments during the period. Just when the show was beginning to gel, I got the call to go to Limerick to play a role in the film *Cowboys and Angels*, written and directed by David Gleeson.

The film was an education for me, dealing with today's youth culture, with all its social and peer pressures, and the use of recreational drugs, and the consequent search for identity. I returned to rehearsals, relieved that I had grown up in more innocent times.

Towards the end of the rehearsal period I had to fly over to the Isle of Man to film a role in a comedy film called *The Boys and Girl from County Clare*, starring Colm Meaney, Andrea Corr, Pat Laffan, Pat Bergin, T. P. McKenna and Catherine Byrne.

This proved to be really hectic, because we were very near opening night, and I was going to return just in time for the final technical rehearsal. Filming conditions were atrocious in the Isle Of Man, because the rainfall was constant and horizontal.

There can be something really splendid about holiday esplanades in winter, but not in these conditions. Huge grey seas pounded them, even spilling into deep trenches which had been dug into the ornamental gardens, as a protection, like great ha-has in eighteenth-century gardens, and there were ominous piles of seaweed in them, making you feel glad that you hadn't been there for the flood.

I had difficulty in finding a flight back home, and ended up in a tiny seven-seater aircraft. A uniformed lady instructed us about the use of oxygen masks and life jackets, and all the usual rigmarole, and we sat waiting for the pilot to board. The lady did some task with her back to us, and then turned, smiled, and donned her pilot's hat, sitting in behind the controls. Perhaps it won't be long before Michael O'Leary, of Ryanair, thinks of the same thing!

The promotion and marketing of *Sleeping Beauty* were highly professional, and the parents were happy because their children were happy. The show packed out.

I can't see pantomime ever returning to the old music hall format, so maybe that makes me a bit of a dinosaur, but what the hell, you can't fight change. I'm available for whatever role they think up for me, though.

— 34 —

Come to the Cabaret

As I have indicated, when I was starting out in the theatre, you had to train on the job. You had to get as much work as possible, and hope to learn as you went along. I was lucky. I got a wide variety of work because I could sing and play the fiddle. I found myself on the cabaret circuit, which comprised golf club special evenings and corporate events. The customary fee for the work was five pounds when I started, but eventually went up to twenty pounds, and, of course, to considerably more, when one had become fairly well known on TV.

But, initially, five pounds seemed like a fortune, when people were working for salaries of ten or twelve pounds a week. The appearances involved long drives through the night, often with rehearsals for a play the following morning. I remember driving a hundred and fifty miles, straight to the Eblana Theatre, for a rehearsal, having risen very early in the morning.

I didn't dare tell my colleagues that I had been doing a cabaret the night before, because this was frowned on by many members of the 'legitimate' theatre.

I was trying to look dedicated and attentive, standing to attention with the script in my hand, when the director said: 'I want you all to take a half hour's break and think about the play, because I have to get my thoughts together.'

I felt that the least he might have done was to get his thoughts together the previous evening, but I couldn't utter a word to my colleagues, lest they might think that I was making much of my ability to earn the few bob.

Cabaret often saved my family from destitution. Just when things were beginning to look really desperate, a gig would come up, and we would have the money to eat.

I went on one particularly horrific trip to Fermoy, where everybody was drunk, and nobody listened. I dutifully did my forty-five minute stint, took my fee and fled to another premises across the River Blackwater, where I had a few stiff whiskies to recover from my ordeal (let me repeat, one drank and drove in those days, and nobody questioned it), and set off for the return journey to Dublin. It had been a heavy night's work: Fermoy and back with forty-five minutes of purgatory, and the whiskies afterwards.

The following morning I woke with the sensation of having a gimlet in my head. I lay on the bed, asking myself: 'Why the hell do you do it? Why do you do it, Frank?' And then I turned over in the bed and saw the roll of banknotes (larger than usual because of the big venue) on my bedside table. I went back to sleep, sucking my thumb like a baby.

One good friend, now gone to his maker, was in the Abbey Theatre company. He was a versatile cabaret artist, playing the piano beautifully and singing. He was dressed in all his finery after a play, and headed for the old restaurant at Dublin Airport to perform.

A member of the company took him aside and asked him in a whisper: 'D'ye not think ye'd be degradin' yerself goin' out there?' This became the code word among the cabaret community. Someone would slide up to you, and ask with a grin: 'Are ye degradin' yerself tonight?'

Cabaret engagements took you to weird and wonderful venues around the country. On one occasion, the late Eugene Lambert, the puppeteer, and then ventriloquist, was performing in a hall in deepest Ireland. He had reached the stage in his act where he would return Finnegan, the dummy, to his case, in spite of Finnegan's heated protests, and Finnegan's voice would become more and more muffled as Eugene forced the lid down on top of him. Eventually Finnegan would complain that Eugene had left his smelly socks in the case. It was a funny act.

After the show, Eugene was talking to the ancient parish priest, who had permitted the use of the hall, and the good man asked Eugene: 'Tell us, the young lad, he never advanced, did he?'

On another occasion, Eugene was in the middle of his act onstage, and there was a Garda enjoying the show from the wings. It was customary in those days for a Garda to appear in the wings, on 'safety' duty (a squint at the show for nothing).

The Garda turned to the singer, who was next on the bill, and said: 'Yer man out there is very good. We had a chiropodist down here last week, and he was feck-all use!'

One has to remember that television hadn't reached many areas in rural Ireland in those days. Indeed, many households in Dublin didn't possess a TV set. Thus, cabaret artists coming from Dublin had an aura of glamour about them. They were like alien beings.

On one cold winters' night, when there were rings around the moon and frost upon the ground, a cabaret group were anxiously awaiting payment outside a hall in a remote part of Wexford, while the hall's owner stood there, drunk with power, with the cash in his hand. He had them all in his grip. They had to endure his endless conversation, and the cold, until he decided to pay them. Eventually he looked up at the huge moon and said: 'Tell us this: what part of the globe are ye appearin' in tomorrow tonight?'

Eamon Morrissey and I were in the middle of a routine in a Wexford pub while we both had a high profile on a weekly satirical TV show. They weren't the easiest audience in the world, but we were getting a reasonably good hearing, until a drunk rose from his seat and staggered towards us. He stood with his hands on his hips, and said: 'Would yez not sing a bit of a song or somethin'? They're getting very bored.' We thought that our hour had come, until he staggered past us, knocked over the microphone, and then fell right through a drum kit belonging to the local band. The drum kit was decimated, and the ire of the audience descended on the drunk, to our intense relief.

I made many cabaret appearances with the late Professor Peter O'Brien, around the country, but one stands out in my mind, because it was so typical of the loveable myopic absent-mindedness of Peter. We were heading for a functions hotel in the back end of Kerry, and as we approached Cashel Town, Peter expressed a desire for a children's proprietory brand of chocolate-covered toffee, called Curly Wurly. He said that he was an expert on Curly Wurlys. You could come across fresh ones, and not so fresh, but he knew a sweet shop in Cashel Town where the Curly Wurlys were always fresh.

There was every chance that Peter was pulling my leg, as he was an inveterate prankster, but it would have seemed churlish on my part to refuse to accommodate him. We pulled up at an unauthorised parking spot, and out he hopped in search of his sweets. While he was away, a lawful parking space became available not much further down the street, and I moved into it.

After I had gone, another car pulled into the unlawful space which I had been occupying. I looked in the rear-view mirror, and saw Peter approaching the other car, clutching his purchase in a brown paper bag. I jumped from my car and ran towards the other car, just as Peter sat into its passenger seat, and pointing to the crushed paper bag in his lap, said to the astonished lady driver: 'I'll bet that you haven't seen one of these in a long time!' Fortunately I arrived in time to prevent her from calling the Gardaí.

One of the most unreal experiences I had on my cabaret travels, was when I was engaged to do a cabaret in a pub, in a village outside Limerick. I was received politely by the proprietor, who informed me that I would have to wait upstairs until I went on to perform, as there was no other private space. We went into the back area of the pub, where there was a ladder reaching up into the gloom.

He explained that the area upstairs was under repair, so I would just have to make do with things as they were. The builders had removed the stairs, and this accounted for the ladder. When we ascended, he reached for a switch, and the area was illuminated by a forlorn, naked light bulb. To my horror, I realised that there was no furniture, apart from builders' trestles (not tables, just trestles), and the floor was covered with thick builder's grey dust.

There was another surprise in store. The wall facing the street had been removed, and there was an icy breeze blowing. I had the violin with me, and various cheat cards, and had still to change into my good suit, which I was carrying on a hanger.

The boss made his excuses, saying that this was the best he could do, and descended the ladder. I could feel a drop of rain in the wind as I looked for somewhere to change into my suit without getting it covered in dust. Then I saw a hook on the wall, which stood out a couple of inches, and hung my suit on it.

I had to place my cheat cards under small lumps of mortar on the floor. There was no chance of checking whether the fiddle was in tune or not. I would have to open it at the last moment. Getting into the suit was worthy of the best antics of the famous French clown, Jacques Tati. Climbing down the ladder with the fiddle clutched in my hand was one of my better achievements. The act went quite well, and I was paid on the spot.

There was still a fixed expression of total shock on my face as I headed for Dublin. There is something quite surreal about being in a room without a fourth wall, the wind and the rain blowing in, and the buses and cars swishing by at speed, with a crowd awaiting the appearance of 'the star' from Dublin.

35

Celluloid

I was playing in a radio show, called *Jack in the Box*, starring Jack Cruise and produced by Brendan Smith, which we used to record in the Television Club, a popular venue for Irish showbands, when I got a call to go down to Dingle, in Kerry, to play a part in *Ryan's Daughter*. To me, this was the chance of a lifetime – my big break!

Brendan graciously allowed me to get a deputy and leave the show. He had been one of the producers of a film of *The Playboy*, which was filmed at Ardmore Studios, and was feeling his oats. His parting words to me were: 'Don't let those movie people push you around. If you have any trouble, contact me. I have a lot of connections in that business.' I would have thought twice before asking him to take on the might of MGM.

My role was that of the 'Lanky Corporal's Friend', and according to the script, I would appear on and off throughout the entire film. The money was enormous in comparison to anything I had ever earned before, and off I headed to Dingle in a state of high excitement.

I was booked into a pleasant guest house, and given a large living allowance. The deal was that I would get a salary of a hundred pounds a week, a living allowance of sixty, and a shooting fee of a hundred per day. I thought that I was right for life. That was big money all those years ago. Each day I had to present myself at the production office to see whether I was required on set, and this I did.

Each day, they told me politely that I was not, and that I was free to do whatever I wanted to. One of my passions in life is walking, particularly hill walking, and here I was, being paid good money to enjoy my hobby. I also love fishing, and I was free to do this as well. It was just heaven, as the weather was beautiful, and each day I would take a different route, or head out of Dingle to where there was a small trout river.

The evenings were spent in Tom Long's pub, in the company of many famous actors, such as Trevor Howard, Leo McKern, and the lovely Sarah Miles. They were all very accessible and pleasant. McKern was a truly well organised person. He arrived in a motor caravan and rented a small plot of land at the edge of the town. What a wonderful arrangement. He had privacy and freedom to roam at will.

There was one English crew member, who constantly boasted that he owned a Rolls Royce, and this was beginning to drive people mad with boredom. He was being given a wide berth by everyone, and was complaining that no one would drink with him. One day, in the pub, he engaged a friend of mine, the late actor Niall O'Brien, in conversation, and was waxing forth eloquently on the merits of his Rolls.

Niall happened to mention that he had done a good deal of motor racing, and was met with: 'Oi don't believe that for a minute! You was never a motor racing driver. You're telling me porky pies, you are.'

Niall asked Sarah Miles for the keys of her Lamborghini. Being a very good sport, she handed them over, and he asked the boastful crew member to come for a short drive with him. They went right through the Conor Pass and back in record time. It felt like twenty minutes or so. When they entered the pub the passenger's face was coloured lime green, and he was incapable of speech. Niall handed back the keys of the Lamborghini to Sarah and said: 'Now do you believe I was a racing driver?' The man never uttered a word, and there was an end to the boasting.

Trevor Howard finished the first segment of his filming, and I inherited his limo, and a hulking Kerry driver, who would sit in the corner of the pub, saying: 'Ready when you are, Mr Kelly.' I couldn't believe my luck. Here I was, a mere cub in film terms, with my own car and my own driver! After some weeks of hill walking, drinking and partying, I began to wonder how long I would be away from my wife and, by now, four young children.

There was a clause in my contract which said that I couldn't leave the location without the company's permission. I didn't think that it would be good for my marriage if I were to be away for several months, so I prevailed on a stuntman, who was going up to stay in Dublin to do parachute jumps in Weston Aerodrome, to give me a lift.

On the day appointed for our departure, he started drinking in the pub, and I just couldn't get him to stop. I was desperate to get to see my family by this time, and I had abandoned all hope of making the trip when he announced his intention of departing. The arrangement was that we were to share the driving, but like all drunks, he wouldn't abide by the bargain, and insisted on driving. Foolishly, I got into the car and we headed for Dublin. That was one journey which I shall never forget, although I eventually took over control of the wheel.

Tex, the stunt man, was to stay in our house while he was in Dublin, and I was taking Bairbre and the kids, who we were taking out of school just before the end of the summer term, down to Dingle in my own car. I had no hesitation in lending the house to Tex, as he was an honest mate, always friendly, drunk or sober.

So off I headed to Dingle with my four children, and Bairbre, who was pregnant. I had rented a large mobile home for us in the town, as there was no other accommodation available. So here I was, with my personal car, and a company limo and driver as well: sheer bliss. We would go for drives around the glorious Dingle peninsula, stopping wherever we liked to purchase smoked salmon (which was a rarity for us then), and anything else we wanted. For the first time in our lives, money was no object.

After a few days of this, it was decided by the production office that I really didn't merit a limo and a driver, and they were withdrawn. I wasn't disappointed. To tell the truth, I was aware all along that the role didn't warrant the transport. I knew that there had been some mistake, and it was a mite embarrassing among my peer group of young actors.

After some weeks the call came to shoot a scene. It came as quite a shock. The scene was used in the film, I'm glad to say. If you watch the film very closely, just after the title scene there are two squaddies shaving in a wash house and discussing Christopher Jones, the limping officer who falls madly in love with Sarah Miles. My line, in a cockney accent, was: 'Christ, that's just what we need, a crippled bloody hero!' But don't cough or drop a contact lens or you'll miss some real art.

Soon after this, the production office dispensed with my services. It didn't seem to be worth their while to keep me on for the entire shoot, and I had to agree. I had done well enough financially, and have only the happiest memories of the whole adventure.

When we returned to our home, we found that it had literally been spring-cleaned. As a mark of his gratitude, Tex had hoovered and dusted the whole house, and not only that, he had replaced all the food he had used from the fridge, during his brief stay. An ideal guest!

36

Ragged Trousered Sailor

A few short theatre engagements followed my sojourn in *Ryan's Daughter*, and then there was a lull. It seemed as though the phone would never ring again. I had contracted a very nasty chest cold, and decided that it would be advisable to see a doctor. To my consternation, it transpired that I had pleurisy, and would just have to go to bed until further notice. This was a terrifying prospect for any freelance actor with a young family.

I made my crestfallen way home to tell Bairbre the bad news, but before I could get a word out, she said: 'While you were out, a friend of yours from Equity rang, and he said that there is extra work going on a film which they are making down in Ardmore Studios, and there is a job going for you if you want it.' The film, *Where's Jack?*, starred Stanley Baker as the Thief Taker, and Tommy Steele as Jack Sheppard, the highwayman.

Now it has never been good for any professional actor's career to do extra work, but things were getting very tight with the bank. I thought that, as my agent hadn't even managed to get me an interview for a part, I might risk it. The agent was known as the secret agent, because he had nearly everybody in town on his books, and he would vanish for quite long periods, taking no calls. Many people felt that he just picked a name out of a hat when a part came up. I decided to take the risk and to go for the extra work, taking the chance that I could beat the pleurisy on my feet.

I know that this seems crazy, but when you are young, you feel that you are indestructible.

My part was that of a drunken sailor. I got it by opting to be tattooed. The regular extras backed off at the prospect of this, but I felt, believe it or not, that my professional commitment was at stake. So dedicated was I that I was prepared to be tattooed for the sake of my art!

It then transpired that the tattoo would merely be greasepaint. I would have to present myself at 6 a.m. each morning, as getting it put on would take some time. The location was in Glencree, in the Wicklow Mountains, above Enniskerry. The film base was at Ardmore Studios, but I would have to be made up at the location. There would be a procession of trucks up the road from Enniskerry to the Glencree location, from 6 a.m. to 9 a.m., and I would be arriving too late for the start of the shooting.

Thus, I would have to take an alternative route, via Rathfarnham, across the Military Road, to Glencree. I found that my early start put me on overtime each day because an extra's contract began at 9 a.m. I was made up by a beautiful makeup artist every morning, who used to put one of her long legs each side of my lap in her efforts to make the final touches. It was a disturbing preamble to an early breakfast before the rush.

The only problem was that I felt very ill with my chest complaint. The costume consisted of a torn shirt of sailcloth, and ragged trousers, all topped off by a shaggy beard. This outfit provided little protection from the biting mountain winds. The scenes were being shot at what is now the Glencree Reconciliation Centre, an appropriate change from its former identity as an industrial school for young boys, run by religious brothers.

The lighting consisted of what are known in filming as 'Brutes', so called because of their huge size. These lights can create a bright daylight effect in the most overcast conditions. They generate great heat, and I used to bake my back under them during the long intervals which would occur between shots. Now, I wouldn't recommend this as a treatment for the average patient, but believe it or not, my symptoms began to subside. Day by day I began to feel better and better, until there was little trace of my pleurisy. I find it hard to believe that I really had pleurisy in the first place.

We had a real eye-opener on the toughness of the film world during this shoot. There was a scene shot in a wonderful Hogarthian street, with open sewers and rubbish everywhere. The effect was terrific. It was like stepping back to the eighteenth century, although you would have to mind your step, because there was a filthy slurry-like substance underfoot.

Extras were becoming concerned about what appeared to be a dead horse lying in the street. They were reassured that the animal was really only doped, and that it would recover soon after we had finished shooting the scene. The cameras rolled, and eventually the scene was in the can. As we were dispersing, the first assistant called out: 'OK, you can remove that stiff,' and the horse, truly dead, was dragged away by a tractor.

Filming moved back down to Ardmore after a couple of weeks, where we were shooting a scene in a smoke-filled, crowded inn. This involved Stanley Baker searching among the crowd for Jack Sheppard, and I was to be at his side with my tankard of ale throughout.

My arm was bare with the tattoo clearly visible, and they couldn't lose me, for continuity reasons. At the end of the day there would be heated argument, in my presence, as to whether they could dispense with my services, but they couldn't, because there I was in every frame with my tankard of ale in my fist, the tattoo consisting of an anchor and a butterfly, clearly visible.

I spent four happy weeks in that smokey inn, in addition to the two in Glencree. Six weeks' work, with a cash payment at the end of each day! At last the scene was ended, and they were glad to see the last of me.

A few days later, there was a call from my 'secret' agent, saying that there was a part going as a guard down in Ardmore, and I could go for an interview if I wished. I didn't dare to tell him that I had been working on the film for the previous six weeks, so I went for the interview with the director, James Clavell, author of such blockbusters as *Shōgun* and *Tai-Pan*. After a pleasant chat, he offered me the part.

I just had to tell him my terrible secret. 'Mr Clavell,' I said, 'I am the drunken sailor whom you have been trying to lose for the past four weeks.'

He looked at me in astonishment, and then laughed his heart out. 'You may have the part, for your honesty,' he said. 'If the makeup department were able to fool me this far, no doubt they'll be able to disguise you as the guard.'

I spent only four days as the guard, and earned considerably less money than I had as an extra.

37

A Friendly Word

The violin had proved useful over the years, not only in plays and cabaret, but on TV in a John McGahern play on BBC Two, and more recently in the film *Evelyn*, as Pierce Brosnan's dad.

Some actors are very territorial about their work, keeping all information to themselves, but this couldn't be said of the late actor Niall O'Brien, formerly of the Abbey. It was Niall who rang me up, telling me that there was a part going in *Evelyn* for someone of my age, and that, ideally, he would be required to play the violin.

'For God's sake go for it,' said Niall. 'You would have a great chance of getting it, and you are just the right age.'

I got on to my agent and asked her to get me an interview, which she did. The director, Bruce Beresford (*Breaker Morant*, *Driving Miss Daisy* and *Double Jeopardy*) was under great time pressure, so casting agent John Hubbard arranged that I could tape the fiddle playing in advance. When Bruce arrived he was charming, but obviously distracted by all sorts of problems connected with the film.

The interview wasn't really going too well, interrupted by phone calls and messages. Bruce was pleased that I could play the fiddle, but that seemed to be the only point scored so far. Then the phone rang again. It was his daughter, calling him from Australia. She asked her dad who he was interviewing, and he told her that it was some bloke named Frank Kelly. 'Is that the man who plays

Fr Jack in *Father Ted*?' 'Yes I believe it is', he said, 'but I have never seen the show.'

'Well,' said his daughter, 'if you don't hire him I'll never speak to you again.'

Bruce finished his call, and then turned and said to me wearily: 'It seems I have to hire you whether I like it or not,' but I do think that he was partly joking. However, the call was definitely some help. The film was a very instructive experience, and Brosnan was most unassuming for someone so famous, but it all happened through the generosity of Niall O'Brien.

My first encounter with Pierce Brosnan was in an episode of *Remington Steele*, which was shot in a number of beautiful locations in the Wicklow Mountains, beside the Guinness estate of Luggala, and on the road beyond the Sally Gap. It was at Luggala that I met with the captivating Stephanie Zimbalist.

She is a multi-talented person: ballet dancer, musician and actress. We fell into conversation and talked about all sorts of things. It was as though we had begun after a comma. I could see the steely gaze of the director from time to time, but reassured myself with the notion that he must have many weighty matters on his mind.

It transpired that she was going to Paris for the first time after filming. Bairbre and I had been there shortly before, so I was full of enthusiasm. I have always loved Paris anyway, and gladly offered suggestions as to what she might see, and where she might eat. She was quite unaffected, and told me that she didn't want to do a 'star' trip, but wanted to see the 'real' Paris, staying in an ordinary hotel and finding reasonably-priced places in which to eat.

I mentioned a hotel to her, but was suddenly interrupted by the director, who had moved up behind us unnoticed.

'Don't listen to him,' he said. 'Get a hotel which looks in on "the court", not the street, otherwise you will get traffic noise.'

We rode out the interruption, and resumed our conversation. I was still vaguely aware of his steely gaze from time to time, but just ignored it. When lunch hour came, she said: 'Let us continue this conversation over lunch. You can ride in my car. Come on, it's over here.'

She had only uttered when the director appeared at her elbow. He looked at me as though I was something odious, and said: 'She goes in the car. You walk.'

That was my last chance to talk with Stephanie Zimbalist. He obviously didn't want her contaminated by un-American values.

The shoot was great fun. I had to follow Pierce down the Dublin quays, and up O'Connell Street, while carrying a shotgun to try and bump him off. The shotgun was wrapped in a jacket, but the effect was so bizarre that I would have arrested myself on sight.

One scene was shot in West Wicklow, in a muddy lane, down which the late Marie Conmee had to drive a Land Rover at speed, with me in the passenger seat.

On 'Action', she took off and accelerated rapidly. We were going nicely when I said to her: 'You're a good driver, Marie. I didn't know that you could drive. You don't usually.'

'No,' she said, 'I've driven once before, and that was a film a few years ago.'

She had gone from first into second gear by some kind of divine instinct, and was unable to tell me how. I told her that the clutch was under her left foot, and the brake under her right. She followed my instructions dutifully, and was able to bring us to a halt by jamming in the clutch while in top gear, and then braking very hard indeed.

By some miracle there was no request for a second take. I can tell you that there is no better cure for constipation than the realisation that your driver has absolutely no idea what she is doing, while driving down a muddy lane at thirty-five miles an hour. I have nothing but the happiest memories of working with Marie Conmee. She was full of fun, and up for any kind of mischief.

38

Hard Knock and Near Suffocation

One of the lovely things about filming is that it gets you out in the open air. Outdoor locations are frequently in beautiful surroundings. Thus I found myself in an episode of *The Irish R.M.*, which starred Peter Bowles.

We were in West Wicklow, at Russborough House, which was the scene of the 'General's' famous theft of the Beit paintings, and the weather was beautiful. There is nothing more pleasant than being paid for doing things which you thoroughly enjoy doing anyway, in lovely rustic surroundings.

There was to be a regatta on Blessington Lake, featuring a sort-out between rival members of two local rowing crews, myself and Niall O'Brien. The battle was to be fought out between us with heavy rowing sculls, and Niall was to be the winner. His scull was to be replaced with one made of balsa wood.

It was a really precarious undertaking for people quite un-familiar with the art of sculling a boat, as we were to stand up in the skiffs and trade blows with each other. I was warned not to connect with Niall's head.

We rehearsed several times out on the lake, and then went for a take, but the opposition's cox just couldn't manage to steer his boat into alignment for the battle. Try as we would, he just seemed to be incapable of doing what was asked of him. The director was becoming more and more annoyed, as the weather was freshening, and the water was becoming choppy. Our chances of getting a successful take were rapidly diminishing.

Eventually the opposing cox got some divine inspiration, and the two boats came into alignment. Niall and I rose for our battle, and sparred with great gusto. Then he landed his victorious blow on my head. For a moment all was darkness, and then my eyes refocused. There was a ringing noise in my ears, and a sharp pain in my head. It wasn't long before a bump began to arise on the site of the impact.

The beggar had deliberately omitted to use the balsa wood scull, and was quietly chuckling to himself, as I did my pratfall out of the skiff. This happy little vendetta probably stemmed from some joke by me at Niall's expense on a previous shoot. However, I didn't harbour resentment.

The following scene was of me coming to the surface of the lake, spluttering. The spluttering came easily, as the lake waters were icy. It was still springtime. This scene was shot close to the shore. My task was to cling to the reeds on the bottom for as long as I could, to give the impression that I might have drowned.

On the shout of 'action' I plunged under the freezing water, and swam down to the bottom, where I clung to the reeds. I stayed there until my lungs felt as though they would burst, and then allowed myself to float to the top. As I was trying to regain my breath, there was an angry cry of: 'For heaven's sake, you came up too early! You'll have to stay down for longer than that.' I couldn't believe what I was hearing. I felt that what I had done was far beyond the call of duty. It was really the job of a stuntman, but there is a tendency on the part of visiting film companies to put actors in situations of peril, unless the actors are strong enough to object.

But I hadn't the bottle to object. I was towelled down and re-entered the water. This time the impatient man said: 'Please try and say down longer. We've a lot to get through today.'

'Action' was called again, and down I went again. This time I gave it my all. I clung and clung until I was almost senseless, and then floated to the surface at last.

There was a cry of: 'I said longer, not shorter than the last time!' On the third attempt he said that he thought that they might have got a take. They would just have to live with what they had got, because they had so much to shoot that day. Somehow, I don't think that directors try that sort of thing out on Hollywood actors.

—⁓— 39 —⁓—

High Noon and Wicklow

I had the honour of sharing a trailer with Ronnie Masterson's husband, the late Ray McAnally, on the film *Taffin*, which also starred Pierce Brosnan in the lead role. Ray and I had always gotten on well, and he had been kind enough to come backstage a couple of times when I had played parts in the theatre, which was an honour at the time. Our friendship had begun when I was directed by him in a play.

We worked out a way of sharing on the first day. It is always good to work out the ground rules when you are going to share a confined space with someone for a while. We both liked music, and we decided that I would bring my ghetto blaster and a selection of tapes to my taste in music, and that he would bring his tapes. Actually our tastes coincided to quite a degree, so there was no problem. Although I had jazz and flamenco guitar and Don McLean, I also had opera and classical music, as did he, and we ended up listening mostly to opera.

We talked for hours: life, art, philosophy, you name it, and it was really stimulating. The film wasn't anything like a huge success, but it was fun to make it. The location was Wicklow town and county, which were besieged by tanned Californian stuntmen, technicians with hammers and chisels hanging from their belts, and us lunatics.

I learned something about grant-aided acting one day, when the car came to collect me at my house to take me to Wicklow town, and I found myself in the company of a young actress, just at the beginning of her career.

We began to talk about the business, and I asked her what she did about income tax, which is always so complicated for the self-employed. She looked at me as though I were E.T., and then said: 'But I only sign long contracts.' I was suitably impressed after half a lifetime as a freelance actor.

There are always funny incidents when the technology lets someone down, and one of these was when the actor playing the chief of the 'baddies' pulled up in a gleaming red car to settle accounts with the 'goodies', and jumped out, storming up the front steps of a building, with the handbrake of the car still in his hand. The car looked great, but I think it had been put together with sealing wax for the shoot.

It was to entertain us again when it was to be blown up later on, down near the harbour in Wicklow Town, and we were all given the usual stern warnings which accompany these technical feats of engineering. No one was to show even the tip of a nose around any of the buildings while the explosion was taking place. Now, this is always interpreted as an invitation by people to have a snoop from a safe distance. After all, it's not every day you see a car being blown up!

We were all duly warned and the fuse was lit. The technicians ran for cover, and we all waited for the ear-splitting blast. There was a sharp hissing, followed by a dull 'phump', and that was all. The anti-climax caused great mirth all round, to the extreme chagrin of the technicians. They never succeeded in blowing it up. Believe it or not, some cars just won't explode!

There was a shot somewhere around the village of Annamoe one day, and I was one of a group of actors being driven along by the river in a minibus. There was a tanned Californian stuntman, named Ernie, in the back, who was stretched out, and thrusting a very annoying tanned ankle and pristine trainer over the seat in front of him. I found it particularly annoying because it was just beside my face. The driver was cockney, with the unlikely name of O'Neill for a man with such a pronounced London accent.

He was intensely proud of his Irish roots, and kept telling us all about various relatives of his in Ireland, interspersed with observations about the beauty of the country through which we were driving. Obviously our Californian friend had not been listening, because he stretched, yawned, and said: 'My God, but this is such a boring country!'

We were all hurled forward as the vehicle screeched to a stop. The driver turned in his seat, and said to the Californian: 'Get out of the car, mate! You are not going to insult my country and get away with it! Come on, get out! Get out and I'll beat the crap out of you!'

We were all stunned, and no one more than Ernie.

'I guess I don't understand you,' he said.

'You'll understand bloody quickly when you get out of this car,' said the driver.

Eventually he extracted an apology from Ernie, who probably didn't want his Ralph Lauren polo shirt covered in blood. It was a silent journey after that.

It helps to be good looking if you are going to play romantic leads in films, and this hasn't exactly stood in Pierce Brosnan's way. One day we were all sitting in the sun outside a pub in Wicklow Town, waiting for the lighting men to rig the lights for a scene, when we saw the tall figure of Pierce standing with his hands on his hips and his legs apart. He was silhouetted by the sun, and looked like Gary Cooper in *High Noon*. He looked truly striking, but the moment was lightened by a groan from one of the actors, saying: 'Ah fuck him! He's good-looking at a thousand yards!' It was true.

40

Another Brush with the Great and How Others See Us

There are two kinds of famous actors: the ones who remain obscenely ambitious, and the ones who arrive at a state of quiescence. By this I mean that they seem to have arrived at a stage when they find their work fulfilling, and don't suffer from paranoia. This is not to state that they have lost their ambition, but just that they don't seem to be consumed by it. A case in point was Michael Caine.

I had a tiny part in the cult movie, *The Italian Job*, as a warder who lets Michael Caine out of prison, leading him down a metal stairway towards Noel Coward, who played Mr Bridger, the criminal mastermind. I had only one line: 'Keep your mouth shut Charlie, you're not out of jail yet.'

Charlie had to emerge from his cell towards the camera. The shot posed some technical problem, and there was much discussion of how to get the shot just as Peter Collinson wanted it. They envisaged shooting a scene inside the actual cell, and this was discussed for a long time. I was left in the company of Michael Caine for several hours while this was going on. I can't remember why he was made to stay in the cell for so long. Maybe he just opted to remain there, rather than to return to his trailer, only to be summoned back as soon as he reached it.

The occasion wasn't unlike being trapped in an elevator with a stranger. You tend to get to know them quite well after a while. He was great company, full of interesting and amusing anecdotes.

Eventually it was decided that they would dispense with the scene in the cell. They had the angle they wanted for the exit, and would proceed as originally plotted. Suddenly, Michael spoke up.

'Peter, I don't think this is going to work unless Frank has more lines. We need more dialogue here.'

There was a great flurry. The star had spoken and the director and minions went into conclave. This all came as quite a surprise to me. I felt that, perhaps I had been the cause of some difficulty. There was a long discussion, and while it was taking place, I said to Michael, 'You don't really have to do this Michael. I'm sure it's not necessary.'

Without turning towards me he said out of the side of his mouth, in his inimitable staccato style: 'Do you want this gig, or don't you?'

It never came to anything in the end, but I thought it so kind of an older actor of such fame to try and make an opportunity for someone he had just met. Mind you, he won't remember this incident, I'm sure. It was so many years ago, and the thing about meeting famous people is that you cannot expect them to remember you.

I have only hit the deck once in over forty years of show business, and that was in a film entitled *O Mary This London*, made, appropriately enough, in London. This dealt with the adventures of two runaway Irish kids in London. I played the part of a priest, who ran a hostel for down-and-outs.

During filming, I was stricken with a painful and terrible bowel infection, and had to be admitted to University College Hospital. It was an appalling experience, matched only by our own overrun A&E departments in Irish hospitals.

I was left sitting on a hard little bed for about five hours, in nothing but a flimsy little hospital gown, while neighbouring patients were being given shock treatment for heart failure, and others were being brought in, suffering from drug overdoses and the wounds of battle.

Eventually my turn came, and I encountered a true professional, who checked me out and recommended medication. She was aware of my discomfiture, being naked except for the revealingly skimpy hospital gown.

'You'll be wanting your pants as soon as possible,' she said, and called someone to get my clothes there and then. She achieved something for me for which some people have a real talent. She left me with my dignity, with her professional manner, tempered with obvious sympathy. I remember her name to this day. It was Dr Jo Dury. On my way out I thanked her, and the male nurse, who had also been very kind to me, and both of them looked at me in astonishment.

'Is there something wrong?' I asked.

'No,' they replied, 'it's just that we're not used to being thanked.'

Fortunately I made it back to the film set in time to complete my scenes. We were working in an actual hostel, and there were three doors in the space in which we were working. Every now and then, a door would open, and a blue-faced methylated spirits drinker would burst in, punching the sky and having an earnest row with himself, only to be retrieved from the room by someone unseen. I turned to the Irish-born hostel attendant beside me, and said: 'Where do all these men come from?'

The attendant smiled sadly and said: 'Ireland mostly, I'm afraid.'

But there are winos everywhere in the world. I had occasion to go to Halifax, Nova Scotia, to appear in a science fiction series called *The Lexx*, which I thoroughly enjoyed, because I have always harboured a secret desire to appear in science fiction. I played the part of a priest (yet again), who ran a pub and gave the proceeds to charity.

The Lexx keeps jumping time barriers, as is the way with science fiction, and so the story can go anywhere it wishes. Sometimes it goes back into actual historical time, with great effect.

I travelled through Logan Airport, in Boston, and up to Halifax in a really shaky little aircraft. The rattles of the aircraft were offset by the fact that a tiny Inuit baby ogled me all the way. He was just beautiful.

Going through Canadian immigration, I was relieved of a hundred and fifty dollars in cash at the airport by an officious gentleman, who chose to ignore my documents, which showed that bona fide employment awaited me, and that this payment was not therefore required.

When I left my hotel the morning after I arrived, to try and make contact with my employers, I encountered a wino standing in the deep snow. He asked me for money, but I explained with embarrassment that I had no cash (thanks to Canadian immigration), and that I had just arrived in Canada, and that I would certainly give him something if I had any money on me, but that I would be passing that way again.

He placed his hand reassuringly on my shoulder and said: 'Do not distress yourself, sir. No doubt I'll see you when you do. You make sure and have yourself a nice day, sir.' Even the winos are kind and gentle in beautiful Halifax!

When I finally showed up at the studio, which was in an abandoned atomic power station, my employers were most annoyed at the imposition of the levy, and I was reimbursed immediately. They assured me that they could recover it themselves. Now I wonder where that money would have ended up if I hadn't complained? Ah well, life is full of mysteries.

My first morning at the studio was not without incident. I received my call sheet at the hotel, but my inquiry as to the whereabouts of the studio was greeted with utter bewilderment by the bright-eyed desk clerk. He had never heard of the studio. It should have been conspicuous, being in an enormous decommissioned power station. I was hoping that the decommissioning had been effective!

The clerk looked at me with bright eyes, widening even further. No, he didn't 'recall' such a power station ('recall' became one of my most hated words in Canada and the USA), so I had to fly blind. There were no taxicabs running, so I had to wander around for about an hour in the snow, becoming more and more desperate. There was no one about in the very early hours of the morning from whom I could ask directions, just eerie silence and deep snow. Eventually I spotted a tiny figure making its way along a road below me, nearer to the bay.

I made my way down, and coming from Ireland, walked straight up and made my inquiry. This produced a reaction of terror, which was quite understandable. There was no one else around, just silence and snow. I could have been a murderous maniac. My potential victim turned out to be one of the most unforgivably beautiful girls you have ever seen. When she unwrapped herself a little, she turned out to be a statuesque blue-eyed blonde, with endless legs and the face of an angel. I blurted out that I was in *The Lexx* and it transpired that she was too.

'Oh,' I said, 'what part are you playing?'

'I'm a sex slave,' she replied.

I refrained from confessing that I was one too. She was most friendly, and we made our way to the studio. Had the desk clerk at the hotel been up to his job, he would have been able to tell me that the studio was just behind the hotel, and just down a little towards the bay.

Halifax has, like Newfoundland, a wonderful frontier atmosphere about it. The sky in winter is a deep indigo, and yet there is much sunshine, which reflects brilliantly from the snow. As in Newfoundland, there is an ethic of hospitality and friendliness. It is situated atop an almost pyramid-shaped hill, so that every street you look down gives you a view of the beautiful blue ocean, with, frequently, a large ship passing by.

41

Communication is All

There is always a paramount need for communication between actor and director in film-making. However simple one's role, one must have the chance to ask the director exactly what he or she wants whenever this is unclear. Filming is an expensive business, and wasted takes cost money. The bigger the shoot, the more bodies there are between you and the director, trying to justify their existence by gazing in every direction over imaginary crowds, and running in all directions to no discernible purpose. Thus, when you want to ask the director whether he wants you to lift a teacup, or put it down, you will be told by a second or third assistant: 'I'm afraid you can't talk to him now. He's far too busy.'

It is far too often the case that if you succeed in reaching the director, you will find that he is really grateful that you raised your query, and will thank you for doing so. When I was playing one of many non-speaking British soldiers in the film *Darling Lili*, some of which was shot at Weston Aerodrome, out in the lush Kildare countryside, at Celbridge, there was a great air of excitement, because there were many old aircraft of the First World War period being used for stunts.

We were all crouched in a trench one day, when we were told that an aircraft would be flying in low, just over our heads in fact, and that the microphones would be left open to get the right atmospheric sound. Thus, we were told not to utter any discernible words, as there were microphones hidden in many of the trees around the field. Several aircraft were to take off, and some of them were going to fly in low, some twenty feet above our heads. But the trouble was that the message was not communicated with sufficient clarity to all of the actors.

The cue was given, and the aircraft took off and headed our way. We were all quite nervous, but muttered dutifully, saying nothing identifiable as actual individual words, until one actor lost his nerve, saying: 'I hope this bastard knows what he's doing!'

This came out loudly through all the microphones, and the aircraft had to be ordered to land. The cost of this was enormous, and we were all lined up in an attempt to find the culprit. Nobody broke ranks, and the offender went unpunished.

A lack of communication caused two further incidents which I witnessed directly, both resulting in serious injuries. One day I was standing with another actor on the set, when he nudged me, saying: 'Do you see that man over there? He is the highest paid lighting cameraman in the world.'

I looked in wonderment at this tanned, exotic creature, who looked so eminent, and wore a velvet taxi cap, allowing his grey locks to escape and frame his handsome face.

Just then, an aluminium ladder, which had been propped against the gable end of a building, was caught by the wind, and detached itself, falling as though in slow motion towards the taxi-capped head. Just as it connected, someone cried: 'Look out!' As the ambulance pulled away, my friend turned to me and said: 'Well, he *was* the highest paid lighting cameraman in the world!'

On another day, there was a scene where a number of actors were supposed to be strolling around sociably, when a wingless aircraft was to make its way towards them. It was supposed to have lost its wings while making a forced landing through the trees. This was a highly dangerous manoeuvre, which should only have involved stuntmen, as a wingless aircraft cannot be steered accurately, being without ailerons to aid the rudder.

Unfortunately one of the actors hadn't taken in the briefing sufficiently, and mistakenly moved towards the aircraft, and had his arm cut off by the propeller. His life was saved by the late Joe Pilkington, who played Eamon Maher in the highly popular series, *The Riordans*. He put his knee in the wounded man's arm socket and, grabbing him by the hair, refused to allow him to look at his wound. Had he seen it, he certainly would have died on the spot. He was taken away by helicopter to hospital, where his arm was successfully sewn on again.

I had been standing around on the set, feeling underused, when I asked the first assistant what he wanted me to do.

'Get up on that roof and bring your rifle with you. You are on sentry duty up there,' was the reply.

I obeyed readily, awaiting further instructions, but none came. I knew that I wasn't in shot, because there was no camera pointing even vaguely in my direction. The hours wore on, and the weather being heavenly, I settled down on the roof to sleep, waking just in time for lunch hour.

After lunch I asked the same man what he wanted me to do, and I was told: 'Just get back up there and await further instructions.'

I did as I was told, and snoozed until teatime. The following day I presented myself to the same man again, and was ordered up on the roof again, where I slept soundly until lunchtime again, and after lunch, until teatime again. This routine continued daily, until most of the other actors finished their contracts. I now lived in fear of losing my lucrative job, and had my meals brought aloft by friends. This routine continued for six weeks, in tropical weather, until I was confronted one day by the first assistant, as I came on set.

'What the hell are you doing here?' he demanded.

'Guarding up on the roof, where you told me to go,' I replied.

'My God, but you should have been gone weeks ago,' he screamed. 'We finished that section weeks ago,' and that was the end of my contribution to *Darling Lili*. It was a pity. The money was good, and the sunbathing most relaxing. Some of my colleagues christened me 'The Fiddler On The Roof'.

One day, after we had moved into our current house and I had undertaken a most intimidating mortgage, facing a horizon of severe cutbacks in our social life, and the future was looking very dismal indeed, I was at home alone when the phone rang. It was Adavin O'Driscoll, head of light entertainment in radio, who asked me to deputise for Mike Murphy on his radio show during the summer.

I danced for joy when I had put the phone down. Here was some good income, sent by God, just at the right time. When Bairbre returned home I told her the good news and she was delighted.

Later that afternoon, the phone rang again. It was Brendan Neilan, casting director for RTÉ television. He offered me a part in *The Year of the French*, which was to be filmed throughout the summer. This was a major joint RTÉ/Channel 4 production, and the salary on offer was enough to pay my newly-undertaken mortgage for a year. I just couldn't believe my luck.

I was faced with a dilemma, and told Brendan that I had a commitment to Adavin, and I would have to see whether she would let me off the hook. He told me that he couldn't keep the part open for more than a day, so I would have to get back to him as soon as I could. I immediately got back on to Adavin, who very kindly released me from our verbal agreement. I rang Brendan and confirmed my availability to him.

The Year of the French was a great experience. I played the part of Cornelius O'Dowd, a rebel leader in the short-lived Republic of Connaught. The plot centred on the arrival of General Humbert and his party of officers at Kilcummin Strand in Co. Mayo, and the ill-fated uprising against the British, with French help.

I was given the use of a mare, named Stephanie, of over eleven hands in height. She was beautiful, and I had the use of her for three months during a fine summer. I had very little experience of riding horses, and was more than a little nervous as I mounted her. She immediately sensed this, and it took hours of riding before she was happy to have me aboard.

What formed the bond between us was when I was annoyed with her one day at Garden Hill Mountain. She wouldn't go through a narrow gap in a wall for me. I dug in my heels and bullied her through, and from that day we were the best of friends. I had forgotten to be afraid.

A lack of communication caused great stress to the producers one day. We were at Kilcummin Strand, where General Humbert and his men were to come ashore in ships' longboats. Historically, the longboats overturned in the rough seas, and Humbert and his men were thrown into the water. The idea was to recreate this mishap.

Men in wet suits were hidden on the opposite sides of the boats to the cameras, and on a given signal they were to capsize all of them, and then conceal themselves under the water. It was obvious that there wasn't proper communication between the men in the wet suits and the first assistant.

It immediately dawned on me and some others that these wet suit extras wouldn't know the traditional calls for filming, which are: 'Speed, Turnover and Action', because no one had taken the trouble to tell them. I went to the first assistant, and said that I had something urgent to tell him. He explained that he was far too busy to listen to me. He would talk to me afterwards. I tried to persist, but he brushed me aside. Then I thought that, maybe, I was making a fuss about nothing. Perhaps the extras had been properly briefed.

There was a call for silence, and then we heard: 'Speed', followed by 'Turnover', at which the good men in rubber suits overturned all the boats, turfing all the distinguished actors into the sea. There was no point in calling 'Action', as there was nothing to photograph, but bodies suddenly struggling in the water for no intelligible reason in elaborate period uniforms.

It was impossible to shoot the scene for quite some time, because the heavy period uniforms were encrusted in salt, and would have to go back to the costumiers in London to be cleaned – and all this because of a failure to communicate!

42

Assignment, Accent and Dialogue

In 2003 I had the pleasure of playing the role of John Smith, the late leader of the British Labour Party, in a Stephen Frears film, *The Deal*, for Granada Television. This was a great learning opportunity for me, because Stephen is a consummate director, with a portfolio which includes *Dangerous Liaisons*, *The Snapper* and *Dirty Pretty Things*, a film which shows the stinking underbelly of the trade in illegal immigrants to Britain, and how horribly exploited they are. Everyone should see it.

He tells you what he wants in no uncertain fashion, but he really knows what he wants, and he will make you do it again and again until he gets what he wants. What is different about him is that he makes you better and better in the process. He is not a bully, and his suggestions are constructive. Thus, you learn valuable things about film acting without having your confidence undermined.

My dialogue coach was the lovely Penny Dyer. I have a certain wariness of dialogue coaches, having done myriad accents all my performing life. It is hard to surrender yourself to the tutelage of a coach when you have always had a facility for accents, but Penny cut through all my prejudices with her professionalism. She made me speak in my best Scottish accent, and then pointed out a legion of vowel subtleties and rhythms which I was missing. It was a valuable, if humbling, experience.

The only parallel which I can draw is with a musician who is listened to by an expert, who points out the places where the musician is not 'hearing' him or herself. John Smith was an interesting challenge for me, because, as Stephen said, he didn't want an impressionist's characterisation.

The point he was making was that there is a world of difference between a well-studied take-off of someone and getting to the essence of a personality, and playing more what the person is about, rather than a caricature of them, and then sustaining this. Penny was unfailingly vigilant and supportive.

My experience with Stephen and Penny was in direct contrast to one which I had on the set of *Miracle at Midnight*, in which I played the part of a mysterious Swede, who spirited away hundreds of potential Jewish Nazi victims from his native country, where many Swedes were running scared, and allowing the deportation of a large number.

I arrived at my trailer full of hope and expectation. Mia Farrow was starring, and I was intrigued at the prospect of seeing her close up. While I was donning my costume, there was a knock on my door. It was my dialogue coach.

Now, I had been running the Swedish accent through my head for days. He certainly was no expert on the Swedish accent, and that is the understatement of the millennium. I arrived on set, trying to rid myself of any taint of the efforts of the 'coach'. We ran through my scene for rehearsal purposes, for the cameras as much as for myself. I uttered my lines, and the director said, in the most Yankee accent I had ever heard: 'You're soundin' too German. Could ye make it more Swedish?'

God knows I can do a German accent, but anyway I thinned some of the vowels a little. At the end of this run, someone, who it transpired was the producer, stepped on set, saying: 'What's that accent ye're doin'? Speak American man. This film is for America!' I have never seen the film, so I don't know what the compromise sounded like. (Maybe I'll keep it that way!) Mia Farrow had the most penetrating stare I have ever encountered. It was so concentrated that, if she ever adopted you, you would know that she was absolutely sure that you were the correct choice.

Getting back to *The Deal*, most of the filming was done in the huge, cavernous, and then deserted St Pancras Hotel. This edifice is of the British Empire Indian style of architecture, in red brick, with the most spectacular turrets. It is an awesome architectural leviathan. There were literally endless curved and ornate stairways, descending to God knows where, with intricate wrought iron balustrades, hung with notices saying: 'Danger. Do Not Enter!'

The sheer mystery of them made you want to explore. There were hundreds of empty rooms, filled with the ghosts of Indian princes who would have stayed there in the days of the Raj. One can only imagine the grandeur of their arrivals. The building straddles St Pancras Railway Station, and dates from the days when rail travel was the height of grandeur.

Getting to where we were filming in the hotel was an odyssey. It took days before anybody could attempt it unguided without getting lost. The corridors were endless and were ideally suited as substitutes for those of the Houses of Parliament.

Our film base was a defunct railway terminus a few minutes away by car, and our trailers were in a vast transport marshalling yard, which looked out in railway tracks behind us. When I was studying the script, it was nice to walk down near the railway fence and watch the trains rumble by. There is something about scutch grass, thistles and railway lines which needs to be painted by the right painter, or maybe I have a bit of anorak in my genes.

The film starred Michael Sheen, who was just completing a groundbreaking *Caligula* at the Donmar, in the role of Tony Blair, and David Morrissey, who had just completed *State of Play* for BBC Two, as Gordon Brown. They were great company to work with, and, of course, are ever-rising asteroids.

I'm not really into power, but discovered that it could be heady if you got enough of it. David and I had daylight scenes to shoot on Westminster Bridge, which required all traffic to be stopped for each shot, leaving the bridge completely empty.

The sequence was shot over two different, but not successive days. You can imagine the illusion of complete power and influence when the police stop all traffic from crossing Westminster Bridge at rush hour, and you meander with just one other person, over to the central traffic reservation, and stop there for a short chat, then stroll across to the other side for another chat, while hundreds of angry motorists seethe with rage, impotent under the direction of the police, and then you return by the same route to where you began.

Don't think power isn't seductive!

43

Television – The New Magic

During my sojourn in newspapers, the new Irish television station was born. I must have created some sort of a profile, because the phone rang out of the blue, with a request to conduct a couple of interviews on *Broadsheet*, Ireland's first TV news magazine programme. This suited me well, as most programmes were recorded during the day at that time. I wasn't completely cut off from some kind of performing, and this was good for morale. I had no sense of guilt about taking work from other actors while holding down another job, because this wasn't the kind of work which would normally be offered to actors.

After *Broadsheet*, there followed some early shows, which were a bit painful, because nobody quite knew what they were doing yet. There was one programme, named *What's Wrong?*, in which myself and Claire Mullan performed various sketches where there were various deliberate technical mistakes, a wrongly set table, or a reference to some prop which didn't exist, and the panel had to spot them. The trouble was that the show was so technically inept that there were several mistakes in each sketch, which defeated the whole point of the exercise. Eventually the show acquired the nickname 'What's Right?'

Another show was called *Meet Mrs Curran*, the brainchild of Gunnar Rugheimer, a gentleman specially imported, along with

Ed Roth, to set up the new TV station. The idea was to take any housewife and give her her own show. The show didn't run for too long, in spite of the gallant efforts of Mrs Curran to make it work. There just wasn't enough substance to it. I have forgotten what my contribution to it was, probably doing some 'funny' characterisations, which were not really funny.

There was a lull in TV work for some time, and then came a request to appear in a semi-satirical programme, anchored and written by one Frank Hall, called *Newsbeat*. It was extremely popular, and ran for a couple of seasons, consisting of serious reports on provincial affairs, principally by Cathal O'Shannon and Michael Ryan, interspersed with actors reading funny letters from participants and viewers to the camera.

Some of the material on *Newsbeat* was really funny. I remember Cathal O'Shannon asking a local luminary in a very uninspiring location in the midlands: 'Is there much tourism here?'

'No there's not,' was the reply. 'Sure how could ye have tourism here? There isn't even a graveyard in it. Look, if I died tomorrow, I'd have to go beggin' to the next parish for a grave!'

After *Newsbeat*, which had been a hybrid show, half serious news items, and half satirical, Frank wanted to do an avowedly satirical show. The reporters, quite understandably, wanted to continue their careers, doing serious news items, rather than go down the humorous route, and so they went their way, and Frank went his. It was a completely amicable separation.

The cast of *Hall's Pictorial Weekly* consisted of Eamon Morrissey, Pat Daly, Paul Murphy and myself. *Hall's Pictorial Weekly* took wings, and its flight caught the nation's fancy. The format was that of a provincial newspaper office, where Frank sat in his editorial chair, ruminating about various provincial and national news stories. As he developed his themes, there would be a dissolve into a re-enactment by us actors, scripted by Frank, frequently with hilarious results. The treatment was always highly satirical.

Frank, being a countryman himself at heart, loved to dramatise provincial court cases. I remember one, where a plaintiff had taken a savage beating on a roadside in County Leitrim. The circuit judge asked him whether he could describe his attackers. His reply was: 'No, yer Honour, but I'd say that they were Rooskey men be the look of them.'

Various characters established themselves, such as the 'Minister for Hardship', which was really a takeoff of Taoiseach Liam Cosgrave, by Eamon Morrissey, and a cruel send-up of one of our weathermen, and one of our newsreaders, by yours truly, as well as a really accurate takeoff by Paul Murphy of Prof. Brian Farrell, one of our senior current affairs presenters.

Frank began to lampoon the inter-party government, led by Garrett Fitzgerald, and his satire was so successful that it continued for a decade or more, with the eventual addition to the cast of Derry Power, when Eamon Morrissey went his own way. Much of the success of the programme was due to the mischievous pen of Frank Hall.

Also, Frank had the ability to mutate the character to suit you after its trial outing. Thus, he wrote two old philosophers for Eamon and me, called Mickey and Barney. He had set them in his beloved Mourne Mountains, but Eamon and I began tricking around with Wicklow accents, which really hadn't got much of an airing on TV before that. Frank took to the idea immediately, and thereafter they became Wicklowmen, with no Northern idiom in the script. Mickey and Barney developed quite a big following.

The making of the programme provided great fun in the studio and the makeup suite, with all sorts of improvisations and coarse humour. For me, the acme was when one actor, seeing the new steriliser equipment for makeup instruments on the wall, said: 'This is exactly what I need. The wife was only talking about it the other day,' and pretended to insert his reproductive equipment into the apparatus, just as Jack Lynch, the Fianna Fáil Taoiseach, walked in, surrounded by his entourage.

Hall's Pictorial was a boon, because it was taped during the daytime, allowing for theatre work at night. When we weren't playing in the evenings, the cast used to adjourn to Madigan's Pub in Donnybrook, not far from the television station, for major happy drinking sessions. I know one thing: I wouldn't be able for it now!

— ∿ — 44 — ∿ —

Children's Magic

Somewhere near the demise of *Newsbeat* and just before the birth of *Hall's Pictorial Weekly*, I made a few guest appearances in the children's programme, *Wanderly Wagon*, which starred Eugene Lambert, as O'Brien, Bill Golding as King Rory, Nora O'Mahony as Godmother, Fran Dempsey as Fortycoats, Aonghus McAnally as the Postman, with Jim Doherty as Musical Director. There were many guest players during *Wanderly*'s long life.

Wanderly Wagon was the brainchild of producer/director Don Lennox, an American who had soldiered in all kinds of television in the US, some of it sophisticated, and some of it primitive. Thus, he was great at overcoming technical problems when RTÉ was coming up to speed. *Wanderly Wagon* was a brilliant concept, consisting of a magic wagon which could travel anywhere required by the plot.

There was that wonderful quality about *Wanderly*, whereby the cast were a tight-knit family without any blood relationship in the plot. This is a great formula for a programme: witness the casts of so many great BBC radio shows, such as *Handcock's Half Hour*, where they all came down to breakfast at the one table, and it never crossed your mind to wonder who was related to whom. Or *Around the Horn*, where people just walked in the door from God knows where.

Don was a most sensitive person, and since the wagon was to be pulled by a horse, he didn't want it to be pulled by just any old horse. He wanted 'a happy horse'. So a happy horse was procured, complete with minder, for the opening sequence of the series.

The day dawned for the opening sequence, and the horse, who was named Pádraig for the programme, was placed between the shafts. All was going swimmingly when Pádraig dropped dead in his tracks. At least he died happy. There might just be some lesson to be learned there about being over-preoccupied with cost cutting.

There were ten Lambert children, and as soon as they came of age, they were enlisted to operate puppets such as Mr Crow, Judge (the dog), and Sneaky Snake. I used to write scripts now and then for the show, and if you appeared as an actor as well, this proved quite lucrative, the performing fee and the writing fee being separate.

Caroline Swift was script editor, and a very demanding one. There were many guest script writers, and she wrote many of the scripts herself. One of the characters I inherited from her tenure was a gentleman by the name of Long John Gold (geddit?). I used to play him with my leg tied agonisingly up my back, a patch over one eye, a crutch, and a parrot on my shoulder.

A couple of years after my acquaintance with *Wanderly*, Caroline was no longer script editor, and Joe O'Donnell was directing. Joe asked me to continue writing, and allowed me to write myself in as a regular character in the show, whom I invented, bearing the name 'Dr Astro', an evil German scientist, who had a little goatee, a Tyrolean hat with a feather in it, half-rimmed glasses, and lederhosen, with mountain boots.

Dr Astro's main mission in life was to bring as much misfortune as possible to the *Wanderly* crew, merely because he was evil, and liked it. Not a lot of motivational explanation is required for very young audiences.

His sidekick was Sneaky Snake, whose voice hissed out weekly (another fee). Sneaky Snake was conceived by a writer named Ian McCarthy, who worked as an advertising executive. Sneaky was manipulated by Noel Lambert, who had to crouch for unconscionably long periods under tables, in barrels, and God alone knows where else. It is a credit to him that he wasn't maimed for life by the tortuous positions he had to assume in the course of his work.

Joe O'Donnell used my scripts quite a lot, until the list of writers had narrowed down to a very few, and this suited me fine. I was very busy, what with *Hall's Pictorial Weekly*, *Wanderly Wagon*, the Gate Theatre and voice-overs: five jobs in the one week. *Wanderly Wagon* was taped on a Sunday, so really it was effectively a seven-day week, and would continue for months at a time. The children were young, and we had many good uses for the money.

Joe was a great director, open to suggestions at all times, and never losing his 'cool'. He felt that Long John Gold had outlived his usefulness, and that he should vanish from the show. As the director he may have been quite right. Maybe Long John was surplus to requirements, but I wasn't too keen on his demise.

He was to be written out in the last episode of the season. The storyline concerned the efforts of Long John to thwart the Wanderlies in all their activities on a desert island. They outboxed him, and the episode concluded with Long John tied to a tree stump, as the wagon flew away towards the sky, with the Wanderlies, led by Godmother, jeering at him in triumph, while the camera moved in closely on Long John's face, twisted in impotent rage, as he shouted at them.

As the camera moved in on me, I had a mischievous inspiration. I stared into it evilly, and growled: 'Never mind kiddies. Long John Gold will be back again!'

The doyen of floor managers, Don Irwin, was standing, just out of shot beside me, but his talkback was open, and I could hear Joe in the director's box, saying: 'Three, two, one. Fade to black. Damn him!'

We were out of recording time and the scene couldn't be reshot, and there were no editing facilities in those days, so Long John Gold lived to fight many another day under another director.

45

Top of the Pops

I had accumulated a huge number of scripts from the *Glen Abbey Radio Show* by the time its three-year run ended, along with various other radio scripts, now of no value. It seemed highly unlikely that *Glen Abbey* would ask me to do another show. Bairbre and I discussed the advisability of destroying them, and we agreed that they should go into the bin. So, with some regret, they were dumped.

One evening the following week, I was working in the front garden when a car pulled up outside. Two young men got out and approached me. They were *Glen Abbey* executives, and they wanted me to consider starting up the *Glen Abbey* show again. I just couldn't believe that I had thrown away three years of scripts the previous week. One of the two *Glen Abbey* men, Brian Swift, who had been most supportive during the show's previous run, persuaded me to give it another go.

After they had departed, I sat dazed in the kitchen. Where was I going to begin? I had destroyed three years of scripts, and although they couldn't be re-used, they might provide some inspiration.

Then the thought struck me that I must do something completely different. I had always been a fan of Peter Sellers' records, and the recordings of the *Beyond the Fringe* team. I loved the thought of developing a surreal, crazy theme to wherever it might lead me, and thus was born a character whose adventures were told through a series of telephone calls.

These alternated weekly with interviews by a very serious BBC Four type, with one Gobnait O'Lunacy, who lived in a town named Ballykilferret. This town reflected all our most devious characteristics at national level. The show was extraordinarily successful, spawning six comedy albums, and a spoof on the 'Twelve Days of Christmas', or 'Christmas Countdown', as I called it, which became the highest new chart entry on BBC's *Top of the Pops*, and reached number one in Australia.

My musical arranger for 'Christmas Countdown' was my good and loyal friend, Jim Doherty, a jazz pianist of remarkable talent, who has played with the world's best. It wasn't beneath him to tackle my spoof. Indeed, the two of us worked on a satirical radio show, called *Only Slaggin'*, in which he had to fit my parody lyrics to myriad tunes.

Jim and I produced several songs together, one of which, 'Charlie Stepped In', stayed at number three in the Irish charts for thirteen weeks. *Only Slaggin'* was justly unseated by the ground-breaking *Scrap Saturday*, featuring Dermot Morgan and Pauline McLynn, and co-written by Gerry Stembridge, who has gone on to direct such films as *Black Day at Black Rock* and *About Adam*.

Life is full of irony. When I was working in the Gate Theatre with the Edwards MacLiammóir company, doing very 'straight' plays, and working in an atmosphere where my comedy work might be viewed askance, I escaped from rehearsal and dressed in a velvet suit in an upstairs dressing room, before sneaking down to Clery's store in O'Connell Street for a lunchtime signing of albums for the punters. My picture appeared in the paper the following day, and no one at the Gate seemed to make the connection.

I performed 'Christmas Countdown' live on the twentieth birthday edition of *Top of the Pops*. It was a scary experience because everything had to be performed live on the show, which was hosted by all its former anchormen: Pete Murray, Jimmy Savile,

Mike Read, David 'Kid' Jensen, John Peel and Tony Blackburn. The show featured Slade, Status Quo and Frankie Goes to Hollywood, amongst others.

I enjoyed the experience, but wasn't bowled over, because I had logged up a fair amount of TV time by then. Maybe I was just a little too old, but I wasn't impressed by the offers of success which were murmured to me by shifty-looking gents at the party afterwards. When I returned home, my children, most of whom were very young at the time, were deeply impressed that I had sat down to lunch with Slade. This, they thought, was real success. Never mind your silly theatre plays!

— 46 —

The Father Ted Adventure

I had been having a very quiet time when *Father Ted* came along in 1995. Work had been non-existent for quite a while, and the bills just kept mounting up. Hubbard Casting asked me to go to their offices for this series about the goings-on in a rural parochial house.

Now, it has to be said that in the climate of Church interference in the civil sphere in which I grew up, the very idea of portraying priests in a humorous context would have been unthinkable. We lived in a country ruled by the likes of the late Archbishop of Dublin, John Charles McQuaid, who seems to have been a very morally tortured man. Censorship was the norm, and until the fifties, writers would have to travel abroad to ply their trade with true artistic integrity.

The clergy occupied a place in society, which enabled them to act as arbiters of everything from drama and literature to matters of surgical consultancy and psychiatry. Long after this stranglehold had weakened considerably, there would have been outright condemnation of a programme such as *Father Ted*. It has to be remembered that, in the mid to late fifties, we were being urged to chase Jehova's Witnesses from our doors (and I mean 'chase', physically!).

It would have been all right to make cruel jokes about Jews and Protestants, but anything to do with the Catholic Church was off limits. In fact, what we had was not just a constitution which recognised the 'special position' of the Catholic Church in the state, but a confessional state.

We even had a Taoiseach who presented proposed Dáil legislation directly to John Charles McQuaid for his personal approval.

I have held on to my faith through thick and thin, remembering (as I said earlier) that it is my property, and not that of any preacher, or even that of the pope, but I feel a great sense of relief at the separation of Church and State which has occurred.

When I was first requested to go for interview for *Father Ted*, I was apprehensive lest the series might be merely cheap jibes at Catholic doctrine, and the commitment of priests. Commitment is never a thing to be ridiculed.

I was reassured when it became abundantly clear that *Father Ted* was really a sitcom about a dysfunctional little family. It has to be admitted that, here and there, it is irreverent, but then humour is always pushing out the boundaries. How often have we heard someone say something relatively innocuous on TV, and reflected that such humour would have caused mayhem only a few years before.

One of the fiercest critics I encountered was an acquaintance who was a Church of Ireland priest. I met him at a luggage carousel at Heathrow, and he was really quite steamed up. Mind you, a luggage carousel is not the best setting for a heated discussion, but he persevered.

'I don't like your programme,' he said. 'The series makes priests look so silly. Priests aren't really like that.'

'I know that,' I replied, 'but that's part of the joke. There wouldn't be any irony to make you laugh if they were really that silly.'

But he was immovable, and I never had a chance to argue the matter with him again, because I heard shortly afterwards that he had died. He was really a very nice man and I am so sorry that we never resumed the argument.

One or two priests remarked to me that there could never be a priest as inept as Dougal, but then it has to be remembered that these characters are caricatures. The whole series has a Beano comic quality about it (a bomb almost has the word 'bomb' written on it). I asked those priests had they never asked each other about a colleague 'how in the name of God was he ever ordained?' and they had to admit that they had.

On several occasions, priests have asked me 'how did you know we had one?' Referring to Fr Jack Hackett. It is a sad fact that with the lack of recruitment to the priesthood, increasingly, young men have had to act as carers of senile priests, who have long since lost the plot. Of course Fr Jack is outrageous, but he is a caricature, and is not responsible for his actions.

Mrs Doyle is beautifully written. She is a programmed, unreasoning, adherent to anything 'holy', but her preoccupation with making tea far outranks any beliefs she might have in importance.

Fr Ted himself is a flawed and lovable human being, who is always trying to keep up appearances in impossible circumstances. He suffers from a whole range of human weaknesses, but keeps battling on with his priesthood. Of course he is an exaggeration. He wouldn't be funny if he weren't! I find his vanity to be one of his most moving qualities, and his meanness is a common middle-class quality.

When I first presented myself at Hubbard Casting, the general perception was that this was some 'off the wall' project, which was unlikely to succeed, or so I gleaned from the chatter in the waiting area. When my turn came to meet the writers, they told me that they remembered me from *Hall's Pictorial Weekly*, and in particular in the role of a crazed county councillor whom I used to play, named Parnell Mooney. (I often wondered was the pub in Dublin of the same name called after Frank Hall's creation.)

The script they gave me to read was minimalist, to say the least. I had difficulty in making any sense of it. We chatted a while, and I had the sense that they were studying me, rather than interviewing me. Then they made a most strange request of me.

They asked me to shout various expletives in the most idiosyncratic manner that I could think of. I thought: 'What the hell! I may as well oblige them while I'm here.'

So I shouted the required words with wild gusto, slipping into what became Fr Jack's accent instinctively. They looked at each other and nodded in agreement, then turned to me and asked: 'Well, would you do it?'

I thought: 'These guys may be quite crazy, but something tells me that they are dead serious. I might as well go along for the ride.'

And what a ride it was! Three years of intensely satisfying work in a show which is still watched daily. Long after my first meeting with Graham Linehan and Arthur Matthews, they told me that they wanted three generations of comedy: myself, Dermot Morgan and Ardal O'Hanlon, in that order, and of course Pauline McLynn was an inspired choice as the housekeeper.

There has been a myth around for some years that Graham and Arthur offered *Father Ted* to RTÉ, and were turned down. This is quite untrue. They never considered offering it to RTÉ, but took it to London and offered it to Hat Trick Productions as a one-off programme. Geoffrey Perkins, a senior producer at Hat Trick, saw its possibilities, and persuaded the two writers that it would make a fine series. Anyone familiar with RTÉ would know that, at that time, RTÉ would never have run with it.

We have to remember the degree of self-censorship which remained long after the Church's hold on the State slackened. Also, it has to be said that Hat Trick was the ideal company to make such a comedy. RTÉ hasn't been particularly successful with the genre.

The surprising thing is that there had been relatively few revelations about clerical sex abuse when *Father Ted* was conceived. They certainly gained prominence in the newspapers after that, but there would be no direct relationship between *Father Ted* and the volume of disclosures.

The Bishop Casey affair had reached the public domain, and was certainly fair game. Also, the late Fr Cleary's domestic arrangements had hit the newspapers and TV, but escaped the satirical attention of the two writers. The antics of the late Fr Seán Fortune were yet to become public knowledge, so really, the point I am making is that there was no subversive agenda in the writing of *Father Ted*, although, in my opinion, it would never have happened without the climate created by a very disappointing Vatican II. If priests hadn't become inordinately preoccupied with youth folk groups, wearing sweaters and playing guitars badly, they might have been less tempting as targets for satirists.

It is much to the credit of Irish TV viewers, and very reassuring, that they reacted to *Father Ted* in such a mature fashion. In parts of the United States, such as Boston and New York, the conservative Catholic lobby succeeded in having the series removed from the schedules, but I understand that it crept back. Good humorous writing will out, despite the prudes.

My greatest misgivings were about the possible reaction of British audiences. I feared that they might seize on the chance of typecasting the Irish as credulous, Church-dominated Paddies, but thanks to the assiduous care exercised by Hat Trick, there was no 'Paddyism' allowed at any stage. They wanted to make a classically funny series, and they realised that any cheapening of the product would have made this impossible.

47

Ourselves

Dermot Morgan was a truly driven man. He always had several balls in the air at the one time, which gave him a constantly preoccupied air. He was really quite a nervous person, and even phobic, to the extent that he would avoid using an elevator if at all possible. His distracted air was often interpreted as dismissive, but I really believe that he constantly felt that he lacked the time to complete all his projects. He was always in a hurry, and had an 'if you thought that this was good today, you had better wait until tomorrow, when things will be much better' attitude. Somehow, he lacked the *carpe diem* factor.

The ironic thing was that, just at the time of his death, several of his television projects looked like coming good, and had he lived, he might have become even more famous. My observations are only based on the experience of working with him on the rehearsal and studio floors. I know that he loved dining with his close friends, and was besotted with his baby son, Ben, and his partner, Fiona. His abiding passion was football. Apart from his constant schemes for new shows, he ate, slept and drank football. He loved Italy, Italian food, and Italian football, and he once told me wistfully that his ideal retirement would be spent in Italy, eating good food and, as he put it, 'going to the odd good game of "footie" in the evenings'. It made me think of Peter Sellers in the film *I'm All Right Jack*, saying of Russia: 'All those corn fields, and ballet in the evenings' – just a bit too Utopian to be true.

I am glad to know that his private life was a happy one, because I know from numerous conversations with him that his work life was a tortured one. He harboured great resentment against RTÉ, and one executive in particular, for preventing him from making the best use of his talents. But then, I know from long years of experience that RTÉ has never had a policy of 'talent management', and I am full sure that the opportunity has been lost by now for it to have one. In other words, he was attacking something which was amorphous. You can't hit a target like that.

So, when I mention the *carpe diem* factor, I am only referring to his working life, and not his domestic one. He was constantly on his mobile phone, and putting you 'on hold', as you stood beside him, waiting for him to finish. This may sound like sheer bad manners, but I really don't feel that it was in his case, because he had all these putative TV series on the go, and as far as he was concerned, any one of these calls might have meant a career leap.

He had an amazing capacity to remember conversations from a couple of weeks before, and he would sometimes say to you: 'Do you remember last Tuesday week, when we were talking? I didn't mean to be rude to you that time. It was just that I had to speak to that guy', and you would have long forgotten the particular conversation.

Dermot deserves great credit for sustaining a difficult role through each series. He had not been a film or stage actor before the show. His forte had been stand-up comedy and sketches, which he did brilliantly, live or on TV, but he slipped gracefully into ensemble acting as though he had been doing it all his life. He was never 'territorial' when you were working with him. If the moment was yours, he would leave it to you, and he often had to do Trojan work in long scenes, and then stand back while somebody else got a huge reaction to the punchline.

He liked to give the impression of being an extrovert, 'laddish' type of chap, but I think that this was far from the truth. He had a university degree, and a wide knowledge of English literature, which he rarely exhibited.

I know that he took a keen interest in my work when he was a schoolteacher in St Michael's College, at Ailsbury Road, in Dublin, because friends of mine, who had children at the school, complained that he used to stop his class at 2.15 p.m. every Thursday, and inflict my *Glen Abbey Show* on them, and he made the odd offhand reference to sketches or monologues I had written years before, when we were working together on *Father Ted*.

I feel that one of the things which made Dermot such a 'driven man' was the fact that he was quite a late entrant to the business, and never seemed to feel that he had enough time. Of course I may be wrong, but I feel that this contributed in no small measure to his early death.

Dermot was extraordinarily generous, and at the end of the first series, gave us all outlandishly extravagant and expensive presents.

Ardal O'Hanlon was one of the most unflappable people I had ever met. He had the demeanour of a farmer on a fair day; always preferring to listen than to talk off the top of his head. I wish that I had some of his stillness. Unfortunately I always rush in where Lucifer himself would fear to tread. He and Dermot would discuss football endlessly, and I envied them their joint interest, being only a casual observer of football and most other sports. Ardal is a very clever person, and very far from the gormless character he plays. He is a graduate of Dublin City University in communications, and has written a couple of novels since the series ended. Once again he had little or no experience of the kind of sustained acting, which you learn in the theatre, and yet stepped into the genre with style.

His father is Dr Rory O'Hanlon, formerly holder of several Fianna Fáil ministerial offices, and latterly Ceann Comhairle of the Dáil. I once dared to test Ardal's political allegiance, and he replied quite frankly that he didn't care what happened 'provided my father has a job'! I thought that this was a fair reply from a son who loved his father.

Pauline McLynn was my lifeline through all the many months of filming down in Co. Clare, and rehearsal and studio taping in London, during the three years of the show, always ready to share a joke. I have a happy memory of one evening when we all adjourned to the John Snow, in London's West End, after rehearsals, and many pints of ale were drunk.

Afterwards, Pauline and I were sharing the same tube train for part of our homeward journey. There were no empty seats, and she and I started to improvise a row between us, whereby I reminded her that I wasn't going to ask her to marry me, even if she had my fifteen children, and she would do well to remember that it was the likes of myself and my father and grandfather who had built this effin' tube anyway. She gave as good as she got, and more. She didn't need my charity, or me, to rear her fifteen children. When we paused for breath there were about six empty seats around us. There has to be a lesson in there somewhere for anyone who is short of a seat on the tube.

I had never seen Pauline in comedy before I worked with her, but of course I had heard her on *Scrap Saturday* on the radio, and this was quite enough to go on. Throughout the entire series, she was a supportive workmate, and as I have said, a constant source of laughter. She and I shared little private therapeutic running jokes during rehearsals in London. In the intervals when we were not required on the floor, we were writing a fancy, raunchy novella, which would have been more suited to an Ann Summers shop than a bookstore. Although outrageous, it was a really funny private joke between us.

Pauline took a degree in Trinity College Dublin. As well as being a prominent TV performer in England now, she is also a highly successful and prolific novelist.

There was a series on BBC television some time ago, called *Comedy Connections*, dealing with what were deemed to have been some of the funniest comedy series ever written for TV. *Father Ted* was featured in one programme, and I was surprised to hear myself described as the 'actorish' one in the cast, or words to that effect. Apparently, I was considered a different kind of animal to the others: somewhat serious in my demeanour; you might say 'theatrical'. This description came as quite a surprise, like discovering that you have a bald spot. Mind you, I can live with it, because it was said with great affection.

I know that I am not really a true extrovert, and that my constant boring wisecracking is probably a defence, going back to schooldays, when I felt that everyone was cleverer than I was at lessons, but then we are all formed by both positive and negative experiences. One of the things I discovered when I was working on *Father Ted* was that there was a definite generation gap between myself and my younger colleagues.

They all came up in a climate of 'alternative' comedy, and had little time for set-piece jokes. Sometimes they would look at me, pityingly, when I came out with an old chestnut, but then that generation mix didn't understand that formulaic jokes are not necessarily offered as 'original work', but rather as a convention, or sort of currency. If people of my generation have already heard a colleague's joke, we laugh politely, and just carry on with the conversation, the main idea being not to embarrass the teller.

I still insist that much 'alternative' comedy, being observations of irony, told in a rambling way over a long period, will eventually be compressed into the formula: 'This fella walks into a pub.' There are some hilarious alternative comics around the world, but this is not merely because their material is good, but also because they are 'funny people'. It is quite impossible to define this quality. It didn't matter that Tommy Cooper's material was at best a series of well-used one-liners. He was a vulnerable-looking, shambling wreck, who seemed to be apologising for his material, but he was just plain funny.

Likewise, Eric Morecambe was somewhat like a successful businessman in appearance, but before he had even opened his mouth he was hilarious. He had a way of looking enquiringly at the audience, as though they were a crowd of complete dolts, and then, with the aid of Ernie Wise, turning the joke around on himself and Ernie without acknowledging in any way that anything was amiss.

I am told that I am essentially a 'comedy' person, and I have been thrust in that direction so often in my career by managements and audiences that there must be some truth in it, although I have tried to avoid the stereotype. People say that I 'look funny' in comedy shows, and at this late stage in my career I have to believe them. If I come up with a good, credible, serious performance, such as John Smith in *The Deal*, they express surprise that I 'had it in me'.

However, as I have written earlier, I have never allowed myself to go down the comedy route as a complete career. The idea just doesn't attract me.

48

Loneliness

It is difficult for a family man, who has always had people close around him, to spend months in a flat on his own in London. At times the loneliness was something which I could almost reach out and touch. It was relieved at times by the company of my son, who was working in London at the time. But he had his own life to lead, and I couldn't live in his ear. His presence at the tapings was always a joy, and my wife and I can still distinguish his laugh in the audience when we see the show on TV. He never missed a taping throughout the whole three series.

My wife and various members of my family came over from time to time, but as I have grown older I seem to need company more and more, and the minute they were gone the loneliness descended again. One of my problems was that the series came after prolonged lean times, and I was determined to eradicate my considerable debts and move well into the black while I had the chance, and the prospect of dragging my body out to Heathrow or Stansted, and flying to Dublin on the Saturday, to arrive home exhausted and uncommunicative, was, I knew, a recipe for domestic strife, and would have been a heavy consumer of money over a period of months. Also, I would have to have been on my way to Dublin Airport by lunch hour on Sunday to get back. All in all, hardly a worthwhile exercise.

I used to try to beat the loneliness with discipline at the weekends. My flat was well appointed, with a washing machine and iron for my clothes, a vacuum cleaner and most mod cons.

I would put shirts in the washing machine on Saturday mornings, have my bath, hoover the flat and cook my breakfast, before practising the violin for an hour. I would then go to a nearby shopping centre and stock up on the best of foods, because one way of keeping up morale when you are on your own is to cook and eat well.

Having filled the fridge, I would go speed walking in Regent's Park, then out through Richmond Park and up over Primrose Hill. Sometimes I would go along the Regent's Canal towpath as far as the Camden Market. It was back to the flat then, to soak in a bath again. Then I would sit down to write a novel, which I had been working on for many months.

After a couple of hours of writing, I would stare into space in a fit of depression, thinking: 'O God, I still have hours and hours to fill!' I just can't take too much of my own company. There is a strange quality about loneliness in a strange city. It makes one feel peculiarly 'outside society'. You are sitting in a pub, idly watching two lovers who are totally engrossed in each other, thinking: 'What a sweet sight', when one of them looks at you, and you have to look away quickly in case you might be perceived as voyeuristic. Or perhaps you are looking at young parents, rapt in the antics of their beautiful baby, and they become aware of your fond gaze and suddenly clutch the infant to one or other of their bosoms as though you were a potential child molester.

I had one almost surreal experience, which made me feel lonelier than ever. One day I decided to read the paper in a pub at the top of Great Portland Street, near to my flat. I ordered a pint of Guinness and then settled down to read. After some time, someone did a very annoying thing. The top of my paper was pulled down very slowly while I was reading. My first reaction was one of anger, until I looked into a big man's face, full of goodwill and apology.

He explained that his little son was an undying fan of the show, and that he was deeply sorry for interrupting my read. He told me that he was a member of the Welsh Guards, who were on their annual drinking outing, and he would love to get an autograph for his son. His courteous manner completely disarmed me, and I gave him the autograph.

I then had the most strange sensation. If you have ever been in one of those hotel elevators which give you endless reflections of yourself into the distance, you will know what I mean. I looked up from writing the autograph, and stretching into the distance there was a long queue of huge men, not unlike the one standing directly before me.

It was a section of the Welsh Guards on their annual Christmas bash, and they all wanted autographs. I had no choice but to comply, and quite some time later I said goodbye to the last one of them, with a dead hand and a pint as flat as ink. They were lovely guys, and all very apologetic. They even asked me to come on their pub crawl with them. It was kind of them, but I don't think I would have had the stamina. I folded up my paper, and crossed the road to the flat, with a feeling of intense loneliness.

49

The County Clare

Nearly all the outdoor filming for the series, with the exception of the first episode, was done in Co. Clare. Our first producer was the late Geoffrey Perkins, a man of impeccable taste and good manners, and if he made a suggestion it was a good idea to take it on board. When we filmed the first episode, 'Good Luck, Father Ted', there was a funfair sequence where Dougal and I were on a very primitive roundabout. I was in my wheelchair, and being an old ham, every time we passed the camera I grimaced into it. During a break in filming, while the cameras were being reloaded for further takes of this scene, Geoffrey sidled up to me and murmured in my ear: 'Just once will do, Frank.' I felt suitably chastened.

In Clare, we were based in the Falls Hotel in Ennistymon, and ranged all over the weird and wonderful stony landscape from Doolin to the Cliffs of Moher over to Kilfenora. Clare is a county which grows on you, at least it did on me. I had been to it, fleetingly, a couple of times, and hadn't taken to it particularly, but as time progressed with the filming, I became hooked on this strange geological miracle.

There is an eerie beauty about the bare rocks, which were covered with soil before prehistoric farmers denuded them, and now and then when I had a day off, I would don my hiking gear and head out over the green road or 'bóthar glas', from near

Lemanagh Castle, all the way to Ballyvaughan. There is something surreal about this prehistoric cattle drovers' route.

As you see it stretching out over the hills ahead of you, it looks like the work of a primitive painter, like Grandma Moses. It is by definition a true 'bóthar', which allows two cows to pass each other without injury. The ancient measurement allowed for one cow to stand across the road, while the other one had room to pass without touching the horns of the first one. In ancient times, a man's wealth was measured in cattle, and their safe passage was of great importance.

Filming was done in the wintertime, so by the time I got back to where I had left my car, I would have considerable difficulty in finding it in the dark. Then it was back to the hotel for a good soak in a hot bath, and down to the bar for crabs' claws in garlic butter, with brown bread and several pints of Guinness. I would then have to phone my beloved wife and try to sound depressed.

The parochial house in the series was situated at Mullaghmore, where there has been pressure to build an interpretive centre for tourists. This would necessitate the widening of the road, which would result in the destruction of priceless flora, which are to be found nowhere else in Ireland, and bring large tourist coaches to this haunted area. The owners of the parochial house are Pat McCormack, an organic farmer and former champion boxer, who is as gentle as a lamb and as strong as an ox, and his charming American wife.

I found him to be a deeply philosophical man, with a true love of nature. We were chatting one day, when he said to me: 'I don't own this land, you know. I only hold it in trust. No one owns this land. We have to treat it with respect, so that we can hand it on to others in good condition.' He also told me that there were passage graves up in the Mountain which are thought to date from 10 thousand BC.

What has happened to our hitherto passionate love of our land that anyone could consider desecrating Mullaghmore with an interpretative centre? What could be wrong with having an interpretive centre in nearby Kilfenora? What we have to realise is that not everything should be seen as a short-term means of generating money. Mind you, there will always be those who will consider anyone who cares a jot about the environment as some sort of idealistic fool.

I was walking on the bóther glas one day, when I encountered an individual who returned my greeting warmly, and we got into conversation about the beautiful countryside. I said to him: 'There is an ancient ring fort around here somewhere, isn't there?'

'There was,' he replied, 'but 'tis in my wall now!'

When I looked at him aghast, he replied: 'Aren't there enough of the bloody things around anyway?'

I bade him goodbye, and put as much distance between us as I could, as quickly as I could.

The logo of our production company, Hat Trick, you will see on many TV programmes, such as *Have I Got News For You*. Their planning was impeccable, which made for a very happy shoot. When people are on top of what they are doing, everyone remains in good humour. Not a little of this masterminding was due to Mary Bell, our executive producer, always kind and full of affection for her cast. Later on in the filming, our first producer left us for the BBC, and was replaced by Lissa Evans, who went on to direct the award-winning *Crossing the Floor*, and *The Kumars at No. 42*.

Despite the filming being done in the depths of winter, we were always miraculously lucky with the weather. On many occasions, after a short shower of rain, we would be blessed by a clear winter sky and the most spectacular rainbows. Should anyone think that they were added by technology, they would be mistaken. Some of the production achievements were truly special.

In the episode where Fr Jack goes backwards up the Magic Hill in his wheelchair ('Hell'), the preparation was a real feat of engineering. A digger had to be procured to level out the pathway up the hill for the wheelchair, and a small track dug in the middle of it to allow for a steel cable to pull the wheelchair. The wheelchair had to be weighted to lower its centre of gravity, so that it wouldn't topple when pulled. In the heather there was a generator and a flywheel concealed, around which the cable ran.

When we filmed the scene it worked like clockwork, and the whole thing was wrapped up, leaving time to shoot another small scene before the end of the day. I have been on many shoots where the project would have died at the drawing board stage, let alone be wrapped up in such a short time.

50

The Perils of Filming

My body double was stuntman extraordinaire Bronco McLoughlin, whom I first encountered as far back as *Ryan's Daughter*. We were all very impressed on *Ryan's Daughter* by his Aussie-learned technique of opening one beer bottle off another, and then throwing you your open bottle. I can tell you we all thought that 'pretty cool' at the time.

He was a most amusing companion, who had been there and done it all. I have encountered him several times over the years on film shoots, and many's the time I have sat on a bar stool listening to his tales.

Life was weird and wonderful during the three series when we were shooting in Co. Clare. Having apparently jumped with the drinks trolley from an aircraft in the episode 'Flight into Terror', I was hanging twenty feet up in a tree for the final shots. The trouble was that I and our director and cameraman were due in Shannon Airport to catch a flight for London, and the time was running out rapidly.

The harness was really hurting me in the crotch, but I didn't complain, because time was of the essence. Eventually I was released, but there was no time to remove the elaborate makeup of the Fr Jack character. I was driven at speed in a minibus to Shannon, while I tore the latex mixed with soda bread from my face, removed the vaseline discharge from my ears, my opaque, blind, contact lens from one eye, and the orthodox one from the other eye. Try this in the seat of a speeding minibus. You will find it interesting. When we reached Shannon, my face was like a scraped cherry, but we made the flight.

Poor Dermot Morgan had to carry so much on his back during the outdoor filming. He was involved in the majority of the scenes, as was Ardal O'Hanlon. Their nadir came when, in a bitingly cold wind, they hitched a lift from comedian Pat Shortt, who was driving a slurry truck, and he pushed the wrong lever, completely drenching them from head to toe in the brown ersatz substance they had used instead of actual slurry. I have seldom seen men in such discomfort before or since.

They had to be rushed away from the scene to be towelled down and bathed, but it was a longish journey back to base. They earned their money by their sheer stamina on that day and on many others.

There were times of some mild peril too. During the episode 'Tentacles of Doom', when the Holy Stone of Clonrichert was being elevated to a 'class two relic', we were filming off a vertiginous ledge on the Cliffs of Moher, when a blizzard struck. It only lasted a short time, and we continued filming regardless. It must have been an amusing sight to see a group of actors grimly acting in front of a camera crew while snowflakes began to settle on them, and they pretended that nothing was amiss, while the wind kept steadily pushing them towards the edge, with a drop of several hundred feet below.

I know that I felt uneasy anyway, because I was in a wheelchair with my back close to the drop. With Hat Trick's luck, the weather changed as though by magic, and we were able to get a good take, so all looks balmy in the completed scene.

There was no way of knowing that the show would be a success until we reached the studio, and the indoor scenes were performed before a live audience, with the outdoor stuff shown on large overhead screens. The response to the opening indoor scenes was good, but when the outdoor scenes were shown in sequence, the audience just exploded, and I for one knew that we were on to a winner.

To Hat Trick's great credit, they never allowed canned laughter to be used to bulk out the live reaction. Thus, what you hear is what you get. If a gag didn't get a laugh, there was none added, and actually, having watched other comedy material since, I have realised that this is the way to make truly funny shows. If everything is funny, then nothing is funny.

Graham and Arthur came up with an extraordinary volume of comedy material. If you watch the episodes closely, you will notice that there are always myriad little comedy moments happening while the main action is taking place, and remember, all these are written!

My favourite stage direction, written in all earnestness by the two lads, was in the middle of an otherwise blank page in the script. It read: 'WARNING. IT IS EXTREMELY DANGEROUS TO APPROACH FATHER JACK.'

It is interesting to note that even the most miniscule happenings were written down by Graham and Arthur. There was minimal improvisation. If you were true to the writing, it worked, and that's one of the best tests of good comedy writing.

Just before the end of February, 1998, I hauled myself back to Dublin on the Saturday, and was glad to be back home again with my darling wife and offspring. On Sunday morning I went to Mass, and as I opened the door on my return I was met by my son, who said: 'I may as well come to the point, Dad. Dermot Morgan is dead.'

It was as though someone had kneed me sharply in the stomach. I had never had such a sensation of shock before. Suddenly, so much of what one had taken for granted was no more. It wasn't as though Graham and Arthur had decided to continue writing *Father Ted*. They had decided to end the show before it became predictable, with the ideas thinner and the currency devalued.

Really, it was the end of what had become a way of life, although this may seem ridiculous after a period of only three years. Dermot, Ardal and Pauline had won Bafta awards and the show had won best comedy award, and it looked as though the glow would continue to infinity. But I should have remembered after such a long career as a professional actor, that there is only the next gig.

There was a funeral service for Dermot in Twickenham, for which Hat Trick kindly flew me over, and I will never forget the kindness of Mary Bell, Louise O'Donoghue, and her co-managing director, Jimmy Mulville. It really was like a big family occasion, and everybody's grief was obviously heartfelt.

Suddenly, every trace of corporate edifice crumbled, and these people gave wonderful support to everyone in their grief. Dermot's actual funeral was in Mount Merrion Church in Dublin, later in the week. It was a huge affair, and was attended by the President, showing the impact that his short career had on Irish society.

I have an abiding memory of a happy day during work on the last series. Myself, Graham Linehan and one or two others were in a taxi, crossing Waterloo Bridge on our way to South Bank Studios, when Graham said: 'Here we are, in a taxi on our way to the studios on a lovely fine day, in a highly successful TV show, isn't it terrific?' He was right. It was.

— 51 —

Scottish Adventure

I was left winded by the wonderful and happy experience of *Father Ted*. Yes, literally winded and numb. I couldn't address the future. Going from the fulfilment of the companionship of the last three years, to the work horizon of Dublin at the time, seemed very depressing, when out of the blue came a call from Scotland to know if I'd be prepared to join in the production of a play called *My Old Man*, opening in the Tron Theatre in Glasgow and touring extensively throughout Scotland.

The company was Magnetic North, and the playwright was Tom McGrath, who among many adventures played for years in bands on cruise ships. After the Second World War, McGrath had played in the summertime for a few years in a seaside hotel in Bray, Co. Wicklow. His play is located in Glasgow, where the hero is in hospital, and reunited with a family he hardly knows. It is a funny, moving and dark play, and was a nice challenge after *Father Ted*.

I had deputised for the host of the BBC morning show in Glasgow on a previous occasion so I was familiar with the city, and I had cycled in the highlands as a teenager, thus the chance of an extended tour all over Scotland attracted me and I said yes.

It was strange, but satisfying, to be back in the theatre again. After all, the theatre is where it all began. It is a very peculiar, physical medium, and can use up enormous energy, even when you are standing still. I am still in love with it after more than fifty years. The show opened for a couple of weeks in the Tron to much acclaim and then we went on tour. The tour was tough, but satisfying in its panoramic scale and venues, including the Isle of Islay and Alness (remember that is north of Inverness!). I had developed a Scottish accent by the end of it.

We returned for stints in the Tron theatre from time to time and this made the tour even more taxing. But it was a great way to see and enjoy Scotland, almost all of it. I would certainly return. It must be added that the play was a great artistic success. I landed home quite burned out, and in need of a rest.

Like most actors, when the rest had continued for a while a feeling of unease crept over me with a flavour of guilt. When does a long rest become idleness (apart from watching one's bank account dribble away!)?

52

A Touch of Class

Just as I was about to panic I received a letter from the director of a forthcoming production, *Die Fledermaus* by the Glyndebourne Opera Company, to play the role of Frosch. I had played the role once before in the Gaiety Theatre in Dublin, so this was an amazing coincidence. I was curious to know whether the director had seen this performance, but no, he had not.

Unlike the Gaiety production, in this one I was required to play the violin. Apparently the director had seen me in the movie *Evelyn*, in which I played Pierce Brosnan's father. In this movie, I had the experience of dying in Pierce Brosnan's arms, and this must have been the envy of many a young woman throughout the country. I took a deep breath and said yes, I would play. It was a very deep breath, because I knew that it would require frantic practice to reach a reasonable standard.

It was a few years since I had played in public. I accepted the offer and began to practice frantically. I was terrified. Would I ever reach an acceptable standard? The best way to play the violin badly is to play it well first, and then you have enough control to make funny mistakes deliberately. Hoping that I would meet Glyndebourne's standard, I set out for Sussex.

Glyndebourne Opera Company is sensational. It comprises the beautiful old country house on whose land the two theatres were built. The smaller, old house, would meet the needs of many a medium sized opera company, but the big newer one is spectacular. The company only operates during the summer season, and the whole enterprise is the height of grandeur. Membership costs a mortgage sum, and the waiting list is truly endless. Among the devotees are multi-millionaires from all over the globe. To land your personal chopper you had to sign a thirty thousand pound indemnity (no doubt it's more by now).

One must wear evening dress to attend the show and there are no exceptions to this rule. No member of the cast may go front of stage in civilian clothes. Formal dress wear is mandatory. Shows begin early and there is a two-hour interval when the audience may picnic in the gardens. Beautiful hampers are accompanied by bottles of the best champagne.

This is an entertainment for the very wealthy, and if you don't approve just stay clear. Leaving social considerations out, I was thrilled by the handsome fee they paid me per show. Opera singers' voices are delicate and valuable, and these international names only perform twice a week. If business is really hectic they will now and then perform three times, and when they did this suited me fine!

Our orchestra was the London Philharmonic, and my playing with it came about as follows: In one scene I am messing around with the fiddle, making the most appalling scraping sounds in my drunken state. This series of scrapes begins to morph into a vaguely discernible Schubert waltz, when I am joined by a quartet of beautiful girls from the orchestra.

The quality of Frosch's playing improves rapidly, especially when the London Philharmonic Orchestra joins in and the whole piece is reprised from beginning to end. What more could a mediocre musical dropout like me ask? I was in heaven! My late father had been obsessed with my becoming a violinist. This certainly would have raised his hopes. Maybe it's just as well he didn't live to see and hear it! The musicians in the orchestra were particularly kind to me and I had several offers of help from them.

This was most generous as they all lived in London, travelling down each day to work. This would have meant a very early start for them. I refused, but one of them insisted, and travelled down several times to help me. He was a great tutor and I'll never forget his kindness.

When we took our curtain calls a Russian-born conductor had to vacate the orchestra pit and make his way onstage for his bow. The orchestra continued to play a march and I popped up in his place to conduct. The comic effect was good, but for me it was a signal honour to conduct the Philharmonic. I then scuttled up onstage for my own bow, feeling drunk with power.

Glyndebourne was lonely. I lived in an apartment in the nearby town of Lewes, not too far from a big Waitrose supermarket. I bought myself an old second-hand mountain bike and ferried my supplies home in a rucksack.

My main problem was with the landlady of the apartment below mine. I was constantly accused of making endless thumping sounds and disturbing her tenants. I knocked on their door repeatedly and never got an answer, even in the late evenings, and they certainly were never in at weekends. My landlady, who was an angel, was constantly receiving angry calls about my unsocial behaviour but was just as puzzled as I was. Finally, I was out walking one day and went away out into the countryside by the river. Suddenly the pastoral peace was disturbed by my phone going off in my pocket, and who was on the other end but my landlady.

She had just had an angry call from my torturer saying: 'He's at it up there now! If you want to hear him you can check for yourself!' When I told my landlady that I was many miles from home at that moment she laughed her heart out. She must have called my accuser back immediately and explained the geographic impossibility of the situation, because we never heard from her again.

I went for many long hikes in the Sussex Downs along the chalk paths. The landscape was a novelty to me. I had never seen chalk hills up close before. The only problem was a lack of company, but the amazing vista almost made up for this.

The highlight of the summer season was a performance of the show in Hampton Court in London. It is an amazing experience to perform in such an ancient, royal and historical place. The surroundings were more cramped than Glyndebourne, but the sense of occasion made up for that. I was becoming tired, much more easily than usual, but I didn't give it much thought. I had always been very fit. Vigorous exercise has always been a priority with me; gym training, long walks, running, hill climbing and swimming. Thus, I was prepared to forge on. Hampton Court was my final engagement with the Glyndebourne company and I soon found myself back in Dublin with my family and my beloved wife Bairbre.

When I had been home for a couple of weeks, my wife and I decided that we would head for the sun for a much needed holiday. We chose Sicily, where Bairbre and I were able to go for long swims in the warm waters. But there was something missing. I was still unreasonably tired and I wasn't able to taste the lovely food that was placed before us. I remember when we went in a cable car up Mount Etna, the car stopped well below the volcano but there was the option of climbing on up to the summit to view the bubbling lava. A few of us took the challenge, and the sight of a real volcano up close was truly wonderful. But once again I was excessively tired when we got back to the car. By the end of our holiday I was quite unwell. I visited my GP when I got home, who referred me to a specialist.

53

A Brush with Mortality

I went through the usual routine for admission and was faced with a most dismissive man, who told me that there was absolutely nothing wrong with me, and to go home and get on with my usual business. I obeyed dumbly, and headed home. The follow day I felt so ill that I went to my GP again. All bodily functions had ceased. I couldn't eat and bowel function was nil. She grabbed the phone in a rage and called the doctor who had dismissed me. I have never heard a tirade like it. She was sure of her facts and her diagnosis and demanded my readmission.

Very shortly afterwards I was readmitted to St Vincent's Hospital where a completely unaffected and outgoing surgeon told me that I had a formidable obstruction in my bowel, and would have to be admitted as soon as possible for major surgery. Hooray for my courageous little GP! She had saved my life by overriding the condescension of a breed of medic whom I detest.

I was very low indeed when I was visited by my surgeon, who had been in the same class as one of my son's at school. This young man always insists on being called by his first name in spite of qualifications which would be flaunted by many another. After my operation he was able to tell me that I had colon cancer which was 'as big as a bag of chips'. I smiled at hearing this, but he was very earnest. 'No, really, it was Frank. As big as a full bag of chips. We had to remove fourteen inches of your colon.' I still wondered, even in my post-surgical trance, how another practitioner could have spotted no sign of such a big cancer. The presence of the young surgeon on my bed in his blue scrubs was most reassuring.

When my wife spoke to me, it was to tell me that this memorable day was our wedding anniversary. That made it doubly memorable, and I promised her a holiday the following year. I remained in hospital for ten days, and then retired to a nursing home to recuperate, before retiring home. I was in no condition to work, and spent most of my time in bed. My condition was a matter of great interest to a loving little granddaughter, who used to creep up the stairs and peep around my bedroom door at this limp invalid oddity. Her little face around the door gave me such joy; I would recommend it as a mandatory experience for patients.

Then came chemotherapy. The only thing to soften the blow was the specialist, who was a charmer. My cancer had been very aggressive, so the concoction in my chemotherapy had to be even more aggressive. Believe me, the effects were unpleasant. Without going into gory details it made me very emotional, and my good wife had to keep me supplied with tissues all the way home in the car because I used to weep profusely. I think that this was largely a chemical reaction, because I had nothing specific to be depressed about. Sure, my savings were greatly depleted, but as an actor I had learned how to survive on very little, and a generous son-in-law had helped me out.

For some strange reason, throughout all the depression from the chemo and the huge impact of the illness, I never thought about death. Not for one second. How was this? I just don't know. I am a spiritual person insofar as I pray a lot, but I am not a clericalist, nor have I much time for holy pictures and statues in quantity. Mass and the Eucharist are enough for me. My lovely little three year old granddaughter Caragh was at mass with me one Sunday at this time and she plunged her little hands into the holy water font with the comment: 'This stuff isn't half as good as the hospital stuff!' I had to explain the sacred difference between holy water and disinfectant. Nice to be reminded that you still have your basic beliefs.

Sometime after finishing with chemo I went for a mandatory scan only to be told that there was a cancer spot on my liver. I was told this in a most compassionate and reassuring way by my surgeon who then booked me in for theatre shortly afterwards. This was just fourteen months after my previous operation and three weeks before my seventieth birthday.

My liver operation was much simpler than my colon one and I was out in a week. There was chemo, but nothing like the previous course. We celebrated my birthday royally. When I had recuperated sufficiently, I was blessed with much radio voice-over work, which I have always enjoyed, but funds were getting really low. It was time for the work fairy to make an appearance.

54

To the Dales

Bairbre and I had attended an awards ceremony in the Mansion House one night, when in bounced the entire cast of *Emmerdale*, plus their executive producer/director. They were having a ball and were really great fun. Suddenly their chief spotted me and approached me.

'My God,' he said, 'It's you! I've always wanted you in my show. You simply must join the cast!' I explained how grateful I was for his offer, but said that I had been in a soap for two years and no matter how good the soap, I didn't fancy such a long commitment. I thanked him profusely for his offer, but he still insisted. I gave him my agent's number, to give myself time to breathe and thanked him for his insistence. 'You won't regret it Frank,' he said. 'This part was made for you!' Bairbre and I discussed this at length when we got home and we decided that I had been out of the running for so long through illness, that I might as well sign up for one season anyway. So I spoke to my agent and she accepted when they rang.

Thus, after a month or so, I was in northern England, in Leeds, and ready to go. There was no sign of the director who had brought me over, but I decided to get on with the work. I should explain that *Emmerdale* is a huge operation. There are ten dedicated studio spaces, apart from all the exterior footage that is shot, and a green room which would accommodate some seventy actors. The whole operation is really very impressive. My producer/director hadn't shown up but I worked on as cast in the current episode, quite sure that he would be directing me in the next one. Then disaster! My producer died suddenly of a heart attack. I would have to see my contract out without my mentor. My role was most uninteresting, and I had to fly home at the weekends for an unthinkable number of weeks. Had I not had the occasional company of my son, Stephen, while in Leeds, I think I would have lost my reason. Fortunately he had business in the area from time to time, and we got together for dinner and a couple of drinks now and then.

Between studio and munching pizza in my digs, I didn't get to see much of Yorkshire on that engagement, but there you are, there are no guarantees of paradise on this earth. When the grand day of my final scene came, the director came to me with an immense bottle of whiskey, saying; 'It's been lovely to work with you, but we never knew why you were here.' At least he was honest!

It was nice to be home again, and it wasn't long before the phone rang with the request that I make a short film for some aspiring young filmmakers. I was delighted to do so, because it has always been my policy to help young people who are brave enough to try and make films. Apart from the difficulty of raising the funds, they must enlist the right personnel and equipment. This is a huge task, and requires professional actors if possible, who are slow to work for low wages, and who could blame them? The request came for me to play in this short film, and I agreed. Their work was pleasing and satisfying, and I was very impressed with the young people's film work, and an end product with a very professional polish.

Over a long period, interspersed with much commercial work, I took part in several short films, and received the most courteous and respectful treatment on all of the shoots. If young people don't get help and recognition from old lags like me then they are not going to get anywhere. A group of friends once got together to make a short film called *Yu Ming Is Anam Dom*. We all worked for nothing, and the production took off and was shown at film festivals around the world, and in nearly every school in Ireland. You just never can tell.

55

Cape Town Calling

A career in the public eye begets some exotic experiences not directly related to the theatre. Thus I was approached by a lovely lady, on behalf of the Multiple Sclerosis Society, who asked me to lead an expedition from Cape Town right up through South Africa to the Drakensberg Mountains. The plan was that this lady and a young and experienced South African man and my good self should fly to Cape Town, and set out from there by car to plan a route for a charity hike.

The South African chap was a great friend to me, and one of the most interesting people one could meet. He had been a newly recruited, but fully qualified airline pilot when the major apartheid troubles began, and was soon drafted into the army. The policy in South Africa at the time was last in, first out. This meant that the newly qualified young pilots found themselves fighting black people with whom they might have had lifelong friendships before their troubles.

It was all too much for my friend who left the troops to their prejudices and joined the Black Sash movement. This was an anti-apartheid movement of women who bravely fought for their cause, depending on a few men to protect them, and my friend became one of these. I remember the day he told me this. We were on the very top of the Drakensberg Mountains, looking out over the huge expanse below. He told me that when he escaped from

South Africa he saw a huge cortège of armoured cars coming from the plains towards the mountains and he realised that he was their prey.

Fortunately for him, his father had been born in the Netherlands and this entitled him to a Dutch passport, which he carried as a safety device. Thus, he was able to make his way out of South Africa through Botswana and Namibia, and from there to England. One area through which he went is renowned for its immense population of elephants. I asked him how he got past them, because they are so extremely dangerous. He smiled gently and replied, 'Frank, it is almost impossible to catch a man who can walk between elephants.'

I realised the truth of this as he spoke. All the armoured cars in the world would not get past several herds of elephants. This man had worked with elephants as a safari guide before becoming a pilot, and knew his business. He now ran a tourist business from London, including African safaris.

We travelled back down the west coast to Knysna and from there he and I went inland to check out an elephant forest. This is an amazing place where the elephants move soundlessly between enormous closely packed conifers, and they have developed their own characteristics, being immensely tall, slender and dark skinned, partially through their habitat and lack of exposure to light, and almost undetectable in their movements. Thus, one can be quite near them without knowing it. I mean, you can be within ten yards of one in the forest and be quite unaware of it. Fortunately, this didn't happen to me.

My friend pointed to the faeces of various dangerous wild animals on the tracks through the forest, and I was most impressed with his skills. Suddenly I saw a huge dropping on the side of a track, and I said to my friend: 'Look, it must be a panther!' He replied patiently and gently: 'No Frank, it's human.' I realised in that moment that I was a city boy. One of the wardens had been taken short. I had a long way to go before being qualified as a safari guide.

Beside Knysna is the little village of Belvedere, where there is a most interesting little church. The glazing in the windows was all brought to the area after the last war, and is the debris from the Blitz. It originally comprised shards of broken glass. Thus from chaos emerged this lovely memento, whose windows are a joy to see.

On our way back to Cape Town we passed through George, where there is a hugely steep valley (truly a 'gorge'). This was crossed by the Boers moving north ahead of the British troops during the Boer War. When you see it you wonder how thousands of men, women and children and their cattle, oxen and carts could have got across this huge steep valley, but they did! It was then on to the wine country around Stellenbosch where we sampled some incredible vintages. There are wines here which we never even see. They probably go to New Zealand or Australia, but they are as lovely as the area which gives them birth.

Then it was back down to Cape Town where the three of us went by cable car to the top of Table Mountain. Then a day or so later we flew home. Remember, this was in preparation for the following year, when we would be accompanied by about 80 people on exactly the same route!

The following year, when we returned with our huge group, one of the things we did was to climb Table Mountain from Constantia Nek on the Atlantic side, where there is no cable car. What brought about this bout of macho behaviour I'll never know, but it was a stiff climb. I had teamed up with a really enthusiastic and chatty guy. It was a steep climb, a little too steep and treacherous. We were both clinging to the edge of a dizzying cliff at the top, when he turned his head as much as he could towards me: 'Are you busy at the acting this weather?' I thought quite seriously of peeling his fingers from the edge, slowly and deliberately, but this wouldn't be the way to end a charity odyssey, would it?

Table Mountain is the habitat of a quite unique animal called the Hyrax. The creature is to be found in few places in the world, and shows us how little we know about evolution. They can be very aggressive, so people are warned to go nowhere near them. They are scavengers, and patrol rubbish containers and car parks in search of food. They have the most amazing appearance, shaped like a medium-sized dog and covered from head to toe in a coat of fur. When dissected by scientists they proved to have the same skeletal construction as an elephant!

They are actually the elephant's nearest relative. This has not been explained. It would appear to show how much work science has ahead of it. Much of the flora on Table Mountain occurs nowhere else on the face of the globe. The explanation would appear to lie in the fact that, as scientists have established beyond doubt, Table Mountain was the only land surface left uncovered during the Ice Age, but the mystery of the Hyrax remains unsolved.

56

Mistaken Identity

Although I'm not a rabid Gaeilgeoir, like anyone with an interest in languages, when I have to learn one – or some of one – I relish the chance. Thus I was truly delighted when I was cast in the TG4 series *Running Mate*. I had the honour of being assigned to the musician Seamus Begley for voice coaching. He was the most helpful and supportive teacher I could have wished for. He worked patiently with me for a couple of weeks before we began shooting down in Dingle, and indeed during the shoot, and I found in him a new kind of liberal and outgoing Gaeilgeoir.

He told me that as a young teacher in Dublin when he was starting out, he couldn't believe the banality of the Irish he was being asked to teach. In search of Irish speaking company, with something interesting to say, he went to a society in Dublin city, which will remain nameless, and he told me that he had never been in the company of so many Gaeilgeoir fascists in his life. He fled.

I feel sure that this experience decided him in favour of music as a career, and what a bonus for music lovers. He plays the squeeze box, and his musicianship is truly stunning. Apart from his repertoire of Irish music, he plays music from all over the world. Seamus opened a door of enlightenment for me, and I would relish the chance to act through the medium of Irish again.

To add to the pleasure of this assignment, it was all shot in Dingle, and wherever I went I was seeing ghosts from *Ryan's Daughter*. Towards the end of the shoot I had some time on my hands, and I went walking over the country which evoked so much of the past. I thought that I would go down to the seafront to try and find the fields where Bairbre and I had such fun when our family were young.

We had stayed in a fine big mobile home in a field down by the sea, but the landscape has been reconfigured since those days, and a fine petrol filling station stands in the foreground, so I just couldn't find my bearings. Seated on a wall nearby was a dumpy little man in a long heavy brown overcoat, his cap pulled down to his nose, and a pipe stuck in his mouth, the original 'dudeen'. At no stage had he looked in my direction, and I thought to myself: 'cute little Kerryman, noticing everything, and not a move out of him. He's just the one I need. He will remember this place as it was!'

I approached him quietly. 'Excuse me,' I said, 'would you be able to tell me where the mobile home park was around here long ago?' He turned his head slowly in my direction. 'For me this is very difficult. You see, I am Polish.' 'The Ireland I knew has changed for ever,' I thought. Perhaps I was right.

57

Hope Springs

The phone rings and it's my agent, Derick Mulvey, with a welcome request for my services as the Bishop in a production of John B. Keane's *Moll* in the Gaiety Theatre. It was an unexpected request, as I hadn't been thinking about theatre at the time.

The call to arms had come from a very old friend, Donal Shields, who I had first met as a child performer in variety theatre with Jack Cruise, and who is now in high-level theatre management. I have the best memories of Donal as an energetic and talented boy dancer, and I'm glad he has achieved so much.

My previous acquaintance with *Moll* was a production in Galway when I played the part of the Canon. It was quite a successful show, and transferred to Dublin's Gaiety at the time, and I was delighted to have the chance to return to it. Here I was, opening in *Moll* again. There's just no telling!

I love the work of John B. Keane. It is mischievous and incisive, and not without satire. In other words, humour at its best.

Our Moll, Clare Barrett, embodied much of the above characteristics and gave a sterling performance, aided and abetted by the veteran Des Keogh as a suitably self-satisfied Canon. The curates, Pat McDonnell and Damian Kearney, were really comical, as was Mary McEvoy as an alcoholic applicant for the job of housekeeper, and I hadn't heard such an enthusiastic audience reaction for many years.

To top it all, we did ninety-eight per cent business, so audiences must really crave John B. Keane.

I had forgotten that theatre could be such fun, but then maybe that's what attracted me to it in the first place, and continues to make me wait for the next gig!